THE IMP-POSSIBLE DREAM

LINCOLN CITY FOOTBALL CLUB 2016/17

• National League Champions •
• FA Cup Quarter-Finalists •
• FA Trophy Semi-Finalists •

Edited by John Vickers
Foreword by Danny Cowley

PHOTOGRAPHS
Andrew Vaughan
Chris Vaughan
CameraSport
Graham Burrell
David Pinegar

PRODUCTION
Alchemy Creations Ltd
Room 10 Coach House Cloisters
Hitchin Street
Baldock
SG7 6AE
01438 748666
info@alchemycreations.co.uk

Printed in the United Kingdom.

ISBN 978-0-9556517-1-7

www.redimps.com

What happened to Lincoln City Football Club in the 2016/17 season was a football miracle.

I am convinced of that. It will live with us all to the day we die and we will be forever proud of what we achieved. We beat a League One team, two Championship teams and a Premier League team away from home while reaching the Quarter Finals of the FA Cup. That wasn't the real achievement though. The real achievement was being able to maintain our consistency in a 46 game National League campaign while enjoying this cup run.

People often ask me about my favourite moment of the season. For me it is simple - the final whistle at the Macclesfield game. A realisation that we had got value for our hard work. From my point of view to see everyone, players, staff, directors and supporters get the success their efforts deserved was immensely rewarding. Whatever the future holds for Nicky and myself, I am not sure we will ever experience a better feeling than we did on that final whistle.

The celebrations to follow showed what a united football club this is. The open top bus parade around the city and the awards evening showed what it meant to the people. It is not the bricks and mortar that make a football club, it is the people and that means our football club has class and it has soul.

I hope you enjoy flicking through this book which is packed with memories from the season. Unforgettable memories that each and every one of us will treasure and look back on with immense pride.

Up The Imps!

Danny Cowley

KEY POINTS: Sub debut for Jonny Margetts & Taylor Miles | First LCFC goal for Adam Marriott | Marriott's goal was LCFC's 400th at National League level

WOKING 1
LINCOLN CITY 3

The Laithwaite Community Stadium | 06.08.16

LINCOLN CITY			WOKING
Paul FARMAN	1	1	Michael POKE
Bradley WOOD	2	2	Jake CAPRICE
Sam HABERGHAM	3	3	Ben GORDON
Luke WATERFALL	5	4	Joey JONES
Jack MULDOON	7	5	Brian SAAH
Matt RHEAD	9	8	Kieran MURTAGH
Adam MARRIOTT	10	9	Chigozie UGWU
Lee BEEVERS	18	10	Zak ANSAH
Jamie McCOMBE	27	11	Nathan RALPH
Nathan ARNOLD	28	14	Fabio SARAIVA
Alex WOODYARD	30	16	Dennon LEWIS
subs			*subs*
Callum HOWE	6	6	Ismail YAKUBU
Jonny MARGETTS	13	7	Charlie PENNY
Taylor MILES	14	15	Max KRETZSCHMAR
Elliot HODGE	17	18	Brandon HALL
Sean RAGGETT	25	21	Luke KANDI

REFEREE: Joe Johnson
ASSISTANTS: Aaron Moody & Richard Morris
FOURTH OFFICIAL: Mike Desborough
ATTENDANCE: 1,592 (407 City supporters)

TEAM	P	W	D	L	F	A	GD	PTS
1. Dag & Red	1	1	0	0	3	0	3	3
2. Gateshead	1	1	0	0	3	0	3	3
3. LINCOLN CITY	**1**	**1**	**0**	**0**	**3**	**1**	**2**	**3**
4. Solihull Moors	1	1	0	0	3	1	2	3
5. Macclesfield	1	1	0	0	2	0	2	3
6. Tranmere	1	1	0	0	2	0	2	3
7. Eastleigh	1	1	0	0	2	1	1	3
8. Barrow	1	1	0	0	1	0	1	3
9. Boreham Wood	1	1	0	0	1	0	1	3
10. Maidstone United	1	0	1	0	1	1	0	1
11. York	1	0	1	0	1	1	0	1
12. Braintree	1	0	1	0	0	0	0	1
13. Dover	1	0	1	0	0	0	0	1
14. North Ferriby	1	0	1	0	0	0	0	1
15. Wrexham	1	0	1	0	0	0	0	1
16. Guiseley	1	0	0	1	1	2	-1	0
17. Aldershot	1	0	0	1	0	1	-1	0
18. Forest Green	1	0	0	1	0	1	-1	0
19. Sutton United	1	0	0	1	1	3	-2	0
20. WOKING	**1**	**0**	**0**	**1**	**1**	**3**	**-2**	**0**
21. Bromley	1	0	0	1	0	2	-2	0
22. Torquay	1	0	0	1	0	2	-2	0
23. Chester	1	0	0	1	0	3	-3	0
24. Southport	1	0	0	1	0	3	-3	0

KEY POINTS: Full debuts for Sam Habergham, Alex Woodyard, Nathan Arnold & Adam Marriott

Marriott
Jones
Yakubu For Saraiva
Yakubu
McCombe
Rhead
Margetts For Marriott
Waterfall
Rhead (pen)
Habergham
Kretzschmar For Gordon
Saah
Miles For Arnold
Miles
Hodge For Miles

LINCOLN CITY 6
NORTH FERRIBY UNITED 1

Sincil Bank Stadium | 09.08.16

LINCOLN CITY		NORTH FERRIBY UTD	
Paul FARMAN	1	1	Rory WATSON
Bradley WOOD	2	3	Stephen BROGAN
Sam HABERGHAM	3	4	Connor OLIVER
Luke WATERFALL	5	5	Mark GRAY
Jack MULDOON	7	7	Danny CLARKE
Matt RHEAD	9	8	Curtis BATESON
Jonny MARGETTS	13	9	Conner ROBINSON
Lee BEEVERS	18	11	Simon RUSSELL
Sean RAGGETT	25	15	Ben MIDDLETON
Nathan ARNOLD	28	20	Jake SKELTON
Alex WOODYARD	30	21	Vinny MUKENDI
subs		*subs*	
Callum HOWE	6	2	Sam TOPLISS
Adam MARRIOTT	10	6	Danny EMERTON
Alex SIMMONS	16	10	Ryan KENDALL
Elliot HODGE	17	14	Ryan FALLOWFIELD
Jamie McCOMBE	27	22	Alfons FOSU-MENSAH

REFEREE: Rob Whitton
ASSISTANTS: Sean Feerick & Tom Hancock
FOURTH OFFICIAL: Hristo Karaivanov
ATTENDANCE: 3,622 (113 visiting supporters)

TEAM	P	W	D	L	F	A	GD	PTS
1. LINCOLN CITY	**2**	**2**	**0**	**0**	**9**	**2**	**7**	**6**
2. Gateshead	2	2	0	0	6	0	6	6
3. Boreham Wood	2	2	0	0	5	1	4	6
4. Tranmere	2	2	0	0	4	0	4	6
5. Solihull Moors	2	1	1	0	5	3	2	4
6. Eastleigh	2	1	1	0	3	2	1	4
7. Wrexham	2	1	1	0	3	2	1	4
8. York	2	1	1	0	2	1	1	4
9. Macclesfield	2	1	0	1	2	1	1	3
10. Chester	2	1	0	1	3	3	0	3
11. Dag & Red	2	1	0	1	3	3	0	3
12. Aldershot	2	1	0	1	1	1	0	3
13. Barrow	2	1	0	1	1	2	-1	3
14. Torquay	2	1	0	1	1	2	-1	3
15. Braintree	2	0	2	0	1	1	0	2
16. Forest Green	2	0	1	1	1	2	-1	1
17. Maidstone United	2	0	1	1	1	2	-1	1
18. Woking	2	0	1	1	3	5	-2	1
19. Sutton United	2	0	1	1	2	4	-2	1
20. Dover	2	0	1	1	1	4	-3	1
21. NORTH FERRIBY	**2**	**0**	**1**	**1**	**1**	**6**	**-5**	**1**
22. Guiseley	2	0	0	2	3	5	-2	0
23. Bromley	2	0	0	2	0	3	-3	0
24. Southport	2	0	0	2	0	6	-6	0

KEY POINTS: First time LCFC scored six in a game at National League level

KEY POINTS: Full debuts for Sean Raggett & Jonny Margetts | First LCFC goals for Nathan Arnold & Jonny Margetts

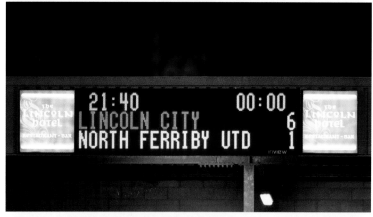

LINCOLN CITY 1
SUTTON UNITED 3

Sincil Bank Stadium | 13.08.16

LINCOLN CITY		SUTTON UNITED	
Paul FARMAN	1	1	Ross WORNER
Bradley WOOD	2	2	Kevin AMANKWAAH
Sam HABERGHAM	3	3	Dan WISHART
Luke WATERFALL	5	4	Dean BECKWITH
Jack MULDOON	7	6	Jamie COLLINS
Matt RHEAD	9	8	Bedsente GOMIS
Jonny MARGETTS	13	11	Ross STEARN
Lee BEEVERS	18	16	Nicky BAILEY
Sean RAGGETT	25	21	Roarie DEACON
Nathan ARNOLD	28	24	Maxime BIAMOU
Alex WOODYARD	30	27	Simon DOWNER
subs		subs	
Adam MARRIOTT	10	10	Dan FITCHETT
Terry HAWKRIDGE	11	19	Chris DICKSON
Alex SIMMONS	16	22	Shaun COOPER
Elliot HODGE	17	23	Ryan BURGE
Jamie McCOMBE	27	25	Joe MORRELL

REFEREE: Simon Barrow
ASSISTANTS: Jonathan Burridge & Sam Lewis
FOURTH OFFICIAL: Alistair Wilson
ATTENDANCE: 3,195 (81 visiting supporters)

TEAM	P	W	D	L	F	A	GD	PTS
1. Tranmere	3	3	0	0	6	1	5	9
2. Boreham Wood	3	2	1	0	6	2	4	7
3. Solihull Moors	3	2	1	0	6	3	3	7
4. LINCOLN CITY	**3**	**2**	**0**	**1**	**10**	**5**	**5**	**6**
5. Gateshead	3	2	0	1	6	1	5	6
6. Macclesfield	3	2	0	1	5	2	3	6
7. Dag & Red	3	2	0	1	5	3	2	6
8. Aldershot	3	2	0	1	3	1	2	6
9. York	3	1	2	0	3	2	1	5
10. Maidstone United	3	1	1	1	4	3	1	4
11. SUTTON UNITED	**3**	**1**	**1**	**1**	**5**	**5**	**0**	**4**
12. Eastleigh	3	1	1	1	4	4	0	4
13. Forest Green	3	1	1	1	2	2	0	4
14. Dover	3	1	1	1	3	4	-1	4
15. Wrexham	3	1	1	1	3	4	-1	4
16. Barrow	3	1	1	1	2	3	-1	4
17. Torquay	3	1	1	1	2	3	-1	4
18. Chester	3	1	0	2	4	6	-2	3
19. Southport	3	1	0	2	2	7	-5	3
20. Braintree	3	0	2	1	2	4	-2	2
21. Woking	3	0	1	2	4	7	-3	1
22. North Ferriby	3	0	1	2	1	8	-7	1
23. Guiseley	3	0	0	3	3	7	-4	0
24. Bromley	3	0	0	3	0	4	-4	0

KEY POINTS: Sam Habergham's first LCFC goal

KEY POINTS: Sub debut for Harry Anderson | First time on teamsheet for Jimmy Walker

DAGENHAM & REDBRIDGE 1
LINCOLN CITY 0

Chigwell Construction Stadium | 16.08.16

DAGENHAM & REDBRIDGE			LINCOLN CITY
Elliot JUSTHAM	1	1	Paul FARMAN
Curtley WILLIAMS	2	3	Sam HABERGHAM
Joe WIDDOWSON	3	7	Jack MULDOON
Scott DOE	4	8	Alan POWER
Craig ROBSON	5	10	Adam MARRIOTT
Matt ROBINSON	6	13	Jonny MARGETTS
Christian ASSOMBALONGA	9	18	Lee BEEVERS
Luke GUTTRIDGE	10	25	Sean RAGGETT
Fejiri OKENABIRHIE	11	27	Jamie McCOMBE
Oliver HAWKINS	12	28	Nathan ARNOLD
Andre BOUCAUD	17	30	Alex WOODYARD
subs		*subs*	
Frankie RAYMOND	8	6	Callum HOWE
Paul BENSON	14	11	Terry HAWKRIDGE
Jordan MAGUIRE-DREW	15	12	Harry ANDERSON
Josh STAUNTON	32	16	Alex SIMMONS
Mark COUSINS	30	23	Jimmy WALKER

REFEREE: Dean Treleaven
ASSISTANTS: Samuel Ogles & Paul Saunders
FOURTH OFFICIAL: Lee Grimsey
ATTENDANCE: 1,399 (247 City supporters)

TEAM	P	W	D	L	F	A	GD	PTS
1. Tranmere	4	4	0	0	7	1	6	12
2. Gateshead	4	3	0	1	12	2	10	9
3. Macclesfield	4	3	0	1	8	3	5	9
4. DAG & RED	**4**	**3**	**0**	**1**	**6**	**3**	**3**	**9**
5. Boreham Wood	4	2	1	1	6	3	3	7
6. Sutton United	4	2	1	1	7	5	2	7
7. Maidstone United	4	2	1	1	6	4	2	7
8. Solihull Moors	4	2	1	1	6	4	2	7
9. Aldershot	4	2	1	1	5	3	2	7
10. Dover	4	2	1	1	7	6	1	7
11. Forest Green	4	2	1	1	3	2	1	7
12. Barrow	4	2	1	1	5	5	0	7
13. Wrexham	4	2	1	1	4	4	0	7
14. LINCOLN CITY	**4**	**2**	**0**	**2**	**10**	**6**	**4**	**6**
15. York	4	1	2	1	4	8	-4	5
16. Eastleigh	4	1	1	2	6	8	-2	4
17. Torquay	4	1	1	2	2	5	-3	4
18. North Ferriby	4	1	1	2	4	10	-6	4
19. Chester	4	1	0	3	6	9	-3	3
20. Southport	4	1	0	3	3	10	-7	3
21. Braintree	4	0	2	2	3	6	-3	2
22. Woking	4	0	1	3	4	8	-4	1
23. Bromley	4	0	1	3	2	6	-4	1
24. Guiseley	4	0	0	4	5	10	-5	0

LINCOLN CITY 4
SOUTHPORT 0

Sincil Bank Stadium | 20.08.16

LINCOLN CITY		SOUTHPORT	
Paul FARMAN	1	Ty BELFORD	1
Sam HABERGHAM	3	Ross WHITE	2
Luke WATERFALL	5	Neil ASHTON	3
Adam MARRIOTT	10	Josh THOMPSON	5
Terry HAWKRIDGE	11	Keil O'BRIEN	6
Harry ANDERSON	12	Jamie ALLEN	7
Jonny MARGETTS	13	Ashley GRIMES	8
Lee BEEVERS	18	Andrai JONES	12
Sean RAGGETT	25	Jonathon ROYLE	14
Nathan ARNOLD	28	James CATON	16
Alex WOODYARD	30	Gary JONES	18
subs		*subs*	
Jack MULDOON	7	James GRAY	9
Alan POWER	8	Louis ALMOND	10
Alex SIMMONS	16	Andy BISHOP	19
Jamie McCOMBE	27	Joe KEARNS	21
Jimmy WALKER	23	Ryan CRUMP	13

REFEREE: Antony Coggins
ASSISTANTS: Simon Wales & Adam Burgess
FOURTH OFFICIAL: Abbas Khan
ATTENDANCE: 2,440 (69 visiting supporters)

TEAM	P	W	D	L	F	A	GD	PTS
1. Tranmere	5	5	0	0	9	2	7	15
2. Dag & Red	5	4	0	1	9	4	5	12
3. Sutton United	5	3	1	1	9	5	4	10
4. Dover	5	3	1	1	10	7	3	10
5. Solihull Moors	5	3	1	1	9	6	3	10
6. Forest Green	5	3	1	1	5	3	2	10
7. Gateshead	5	3	0	2	14	5	9	9
8. LINCOLN CITY	**5**	**3**	**0**	**2**	**14**	**6**	**8**	**9**
9. Macclesfield	5	3	0	2	8	5	3	9
10. Boreham Wood	5	2	2	1	7	4	3	8
11. Wrexham	5	2	2	1	4	4	0	8
12. Maidstone United	5	2	1	2	7	6	1	7
13. Aldershot	5	2	1	2	5	5	0	7
14. Barrow	5	2	1	2	6	8	-2	7
15. North Ferriby	5	2	1	2	5	10	-5	7
16. Braintree	5	1	2	2	5	6	-1	5
17. Eastleigh	5	1	2	2	6	8	-2	5
18. York	5	1	2	2	5	10	-5	5
19. Chester	5	1	1	3	7	10	-3	4
20. Bromley	5	1	1	3	5	8	-3	4
21. Torquay	5	1	1	3	2	6	-4	4
22. SOUTHPORT	**5**	**1**	**0**	**4**	**3**	**14**	**-11**	**3**
23. Woking	5	0	1	4	5	11	-6	1
24. Guiseley	5	0	0	5	7	13	-6	0

KEY POINTS: Full debut for Harry Anderson | Terry Hawkridge had a 58th minute penalty saved

KEY POINTS: Harry Anderson's first LCFC goal

MACCLESFIELD TOWN 1
LINCOLN CITY 2

Moss Rose Ground | 27.08.16

MACCLESFIELD TOWN		LINCOLN CITY	
Ritchie BRANAGAN	1	1	Paul FARMAN
David FITZPATRICK	3	3	Sam HABERGHAM
George PILKINGTON	5	5	Luke WATERFALL
John McCOMBE	6	9	Matt RHEAD
Paul LEWIS	8	11	Terry HAWKRIDGE
Chris HOLROYD	9	12	Harry ANDERSON
Jack SAMPSON	10	13	Jonny MARGETTS
Danny ROWE	11	18	Lee BEEVERS
Dan COWAN	12	27	Jamie McCOMBE
Kingsley JAMES	14	28	Nathan ARNOLD
Danny WHITAKER	23	30	Alex WOODYARD
subs		subs	
Neill BYRNE	4	8	Alan POWER
Jack MACKRETH	7	10	Adam MARRIOTT
Ollie NORBURN	15	16	Alex SIMMONS
Mitch HANCOX	16	25	Sean RAGGETT
Craig ROSS	13	23	Jimmy WALKER

REFEREE: Andrew Miller
ASSISTANTS: Richard Watson & Simon Brown
FOURTH OFFICIAL: Kenwyn Hughes
ATTENDANCE: 1,615 (380 City supporters)

TEAM	P	W	D	L	F	A	GD	PTS
1. Tranmere	6	5	1	0	10	3	7	16
2. Dag & Red	6	5	0	1	12	4	8	15
3. Forest Green	6	4	1	1	9	4	5	13
4. LINCOLN CITY	**6**	**4**	**0**	**2**	**16**	**7**	**9**	**12**
5. Gateshead	6	3	1	2	15	6	9	10
6. Dover	6	3	1	2	11	9	2	10
7. Aldershot	6	3	1	2	7	5	2	10
8. Solihull Moors	6	3	1	2	9	8	1	10
9. Sutton United	6	3	1	2	9	9	0	10
10. Barrow	6	3	1	2	8	9	-1	10
11. Boreham Wood	6	2	3	1	8	5	3	9
12. MACCLESFIELD	**6**	**3**	**0**	**3**	**9**	**7**	**2**	**9**
13. Eastleigh	6	2	2	2	8	8	0	8
14. York	6	2	2	2	9	11	-2	8
15. Wrexham	6	2	2	2	4	7	-3	8
16. Chester	6	2	1	3	11	10	1	7
17. Bromley	6	2	1	3	9	9	0	7
18. Maidstone United	6	2	1	3	8	10	-2	7
19. Torquay	6	2	1	3	4	7	-3	7
20. North Ferriby	6	2	1	3	5	12	-7	7
21. Braintree	6	1	2	3	6	8	-2	5
22. Southport	6	1	1	4	4	15	-11	4
23. Woking	6	0	1	5	6	15	-9	1
24. Guiseley	6	0	0	6	8	17	-9	0

McCombe

Whitaker

James · Sampson · Farman

Byrne for McCombe

Anderson

Power for Arnold

Marriott for Rhead · Norburn for Whitaker

Marriott

Marriott

Mackreth for Lewis

LINCOLN CITY 3
GATESHEAD 0

Sincil Bank Stadium | 29.08.16

LINCOLN CITY			GATESHEAD
Paul FARMAN	1	1	Sam JOHNSON
Bradley WOOD	2	2	James BOLTON
Sam HABERGHAM	3	3	George SMITH
Luke WATERFALL	5	4	Manny SMITH
Matt RHEAD	9	5	Liam HOGAN
Adam MARRIOTT	10	6	Jamal FYFIELD
Harry ANDERSON	12	7	Wes YORK
Lee BEEVERS	18	9	Danny JOHNSON
Sean RAGGETT	25	19	Ryan BOWMAN
Nathan ARNOLD	28	22	Gus MAFUTA
Alex WOODYARD	30	26	Paddy McLAUGHLIN
subs		subs	
Alan POWER	8	8	Mitch BRUNDLE
Terry HAWKRIDGE	11	10	Sam JONES
Jonny MARGETTS	13	14	Toby AJALA
Jamie McCOMBE	27	17	Reece STYCHE
Jimmy WALKER	23	13	Dan HANFORD

REFEREE: Thomas Bramall
ASSISTANTS: Martyn Holmes & Alex Guy
FOURTH OFFICIAL: James Turner
ATTENDANCE: 3,687 (110 visiting supporters)

TEAM	P	W	D	L	F	A	GD	PTS
1. Tranmere	7	6	1	0	11	3	8	19
2. Forest Green	7	5	1	1	14	5	9	16
3. LINCOLN CITY	**7**	**5**	**0**	**2**	**19**	**7**	**12**	**15**
4. Dag & Red	7	5	0	2	12	5	7	15
5. Aldershot	7	4	1	2	9	6	3	13
6. Sutton United	7	4	1	2	10	9	1	13
7. Barrow	7	4	1	2	9	9	0	13
8. Macclesfield	7	4	0	3	12	9	3	12
9. Eastleigh	7	3	2	2	13	8	5	11
10. Wrexham	7	3	2	2	6	8	-2	11
11. GATESHEAD	**7**	**3**	**1**	**3**	**15**	**9**	**6**	**10**
12. Dover	7	3	1	3	12	11	1	10
13. Solihull Moors	7	3	1	3	11	11	0	10
14. Maidstone United	7	3	1	3	9	10	-1	10
15. Torquay	7	3	1	3	7	8	-1	10
16. Boreham Wood	7	2	3	2	8	6	2	9
17. York	7	2	2	3	10	13	-3	8
18. Chester	7	2	1	4	12	13	-1	7
19. Bromley	7	2	1	4	9	14	-5	7
20. North Ferriby	7	2	1	4	5	13	-8	7
21. Braintree	7	1	2	4	7	11	-4	5
22. Woking	7	1	1	5	9	16	-7	4
23. Southport	7	1	1	5	5	20	-15	4
24. Guiseley	7	0	0	7	8	18	-10	0

Raggett

Arnold

G Smith
Ajala for G Smith

Styche for Bowman

Margetts for Rhead

Jones for Johnson

Hawkridge for Arnold

Marriott   Power for Marriott

Hawkridge   M Smith

1 2 3 4 5 6 7 8 9 10 11 12 13 14 15 16 17 18 19 20 21 22 23 24 25 26 27 28 29 30 31 32 33 34 35 36 37 38 39 40 41 42 43 44 45 46 47 48 49 50 51 52 53 54 55 56 57 58 59 60 61 62 63 64 65 66 67 68 69 70 71 72 73 74 75 76 77 78 79 80 81 82 83 84 85 86 87 88 89 90

KEY POINTS: Sean Raggett's first LCFC goal

KEY POINTS: Game televised live on BT Sport | Kick-off time 5.30pm | Sub debut for Macauley Bonne

TORQUAY UNITED 1
LINCOLN CITY 2
Plainmoor | 03.09.16

TORQUAY UNITED			LINCOLN CITY
Brendan MOORE	1	1	Paul FARMAN
Lathaniel ROWE-TURNER	3	2	Bradley WOOD
Giancarlo GALLIFUOCO	5	3	Sam HABERGHAM
Luke YOUNG	8	5	Luke WATERFALL
Nathan BLISSETT	9	9	Matt RHEAD
Courtney RICHARDS	10	10	Adam MARRIOTT
Dan SPARKES	11	12	Harry ANDERSON
Aman VERMA	12	18	Lee BEEVERS
Sean McGINTY	15	25	Sean RAGGETT
Jamie REID	18	28	Nathan ARNOLD
Joe WARD	19	30	Alex WOODYARD
subs			*subs*
Ben GERRING	6	8	Alan POWER
Sam CHANEY	7	11	Terry HAWKRIDGE
Brett WILLIAMS	14	27	Jamie McCOMBE
Chay SCRIVENS	17	29	Macauley BONNE
Jamie CHAMBERLAIN	29	23	Jimmy WALKER

REFEREE: Craig Hicks
ASSISTANTS: Samuel Ogles & Alex Blake
FOURTH OFFICIAL: Samuel Allison
ATTENDANCE: 2,061 (173 City supporters)

TEAM	P	W	D	L	F	A	GD	PTS
1. Forest Green	8	6	1	1	16	6	10	19
2. Tranmere	8	6	1	1	12	6	6	19
3. LINCOLN CITY	**8**	**6**	**0**	**2**	**21**	**8**	**13**	**18**
4. Aldershot	8	5	1	2	12	7	5	16
5. Macclesfield	8	5	0	3	15	10	5	15
6. Dag & Red	8	5	0	3	12	7	5	15
7. Eastleigh	8	4	2	2	15	8	7	14
8. Barrow	8	4	2	2	10	10	0	14
9. Gateshead	8	4	1	3	16	9	7	13
10. Dover	8	4	1	3	13	11	2	13
11. Sutton United	8	4	1	3	10	10	0	13
12. Boreham Wood	8	3	3	2	10	6	4	12
13. Wrexham	8	3	3	2	8	10	-2	12
14. York	8	3	2	3	14	13	1	11
15. Maidstone United	8	3	2	3	11	12	-1	11
16. TORQUAY	**8**	**3**	**1**	**4**	**8**	**10**	**-2**	**10**
17. Solihull Moors	8	3	1	4	11	15	-4	10
18. Bromley	8	2	2	4	10	15	-5	8
19. Chester	8	2	1	5	13	15	-2	7
20. North Ferriby	8	2	1	5	5	15	-10	7
21. Braintree	8	1	3	4	7	11	-4	6
22. Woking	8	1	1	6	10	19	-9	4
23. Southport	8	1	1	6	5	21	-16	4
24. Guiseley	8	0	1	7	8	18	-10	1

KEY POINTS: Full debut for Macauley Bonne | Macauley Bonne's first LCFC goal

TRANMERE ROVERS 0
LINCOLN CITY 1

Prenton Park | 10.09.16

TRANMERE ROVERS			LINCOLN CITY
Scott DAVIES	1	1	Paul FARMAN
Lee VAUGHAN	2	2	Bradley WOOD
Steve JENNINGS	4	3	Sam HABERGHAM
Steve McNULTY	5	5	Luke WATERFALL
Michael IHIEKWE	6	9	Matt RHEAD
Jay HARRIS	8	11	Terry HAWKRIDGE
Andy COOK	9	18	Lee BEEVERS
James NORWOOD	10	25	Sean RAGGETT
Connor JENNINGS	11	28	Nathan ARNOLD
Lois MAYNARD	20	29	Macauley BONNE
Jeff HUGHES	24	30	Alex WOODYARD
subs		*subs*	
Liam RIDEHALGH	3	7	Jack MULDOON
Adam MEKKI	7	8	Alan POWER
Darren STEPHENSON	14	10	Adam MARRIOTT
Jake KIRBY	17	12	Harry ANDERSON
Iain TURNER	13	27	Jamie McCOMBE

REFEREE: Martin Coy
ASSISTANTS: Peter Sporne & John Matthews
FOURTH OFFICIAL: Oliver Bickle
ATTENDANCE: 5,274 (540 City supporters)

TEAM	P	W	D	L	F	A	GD	PTS
1. LINCOLN CITY	9	7	0	2	22	8	14	21
2. Forest Green	9	6	1	2	19	10	9	19
3. TRANMERE	9	6	1	2	12	7	5	19
4. Dag & Red	9	6	0	3	17	9	8	18
5. Macclesfield	9	6	0	3	16	10	6	18
6. Aldershot	9	5	2	2	12	7	5	17
7. Gateshead	9	5	1	3	20	10	10	16
8. Dover	9	5	1	3	17	14	3	16
9. Eastleigh	9	4	3	2	16	9	7	15
10. Barrow	9	4	3	2	11	11	0	15
11. Wrexham	9	4	3	2	9	10	-1	15
12. Maidstone United	9	4	2	3	13	12	1	14
13. Boreham Wood	9	3	4	2	11	7	4	13
14. Torquay	9	4	1	4	10	10	0	13
15. Sutton United	9	4	1	4	10	11	-1	13
16. York	9	3	2	4	14	15	-1	11
17. Solihull Moors	9	3	1	5	13	20	-7	10
18. Chester	9	2	2	5	13	15	-2	8
19. Bromley	9	2	2	5	10	16	-6	8
20. North Ferriby	9	2	1	6	5	17	-12	7
21. Braintree	9	1	3	5	8	15	-7	6
22. Woking	9	1	2	6	11	20	-9	5
23. Southport	9	1	2	6	6	22	-16	5
24. Guiseley	9	0	2	7	9	19	-10	2

Harris | Kirby for C Jennings / Wood | McNulty | Anderson for Arnold | Bonne | Stephenson for Cook | Marriott for Bonne | Power for Wood | Mekki for Harris | Farman | Hawkridge

LINCOLN CITY 0
SOLIHULL MOORS 0

Sincil Bank Stadium | 13.09.16

LINCOLN CITY		SOLIHULL MOORS	
Paul FARMAN	1	23	Nathan VAUGHAN
Bradley WOOD	2	2	Shepherd MUROMBEDZI
Sam HABERGHAM	3	3	Connor FRANKLIN
Luke WATERFALL	5	4	Liam DALY
Matt RHEAD	9	10	Ryan BESWICK
Adam MARRIOTT	10	11	Darryl KNIGHTS
Terry HAWKRIDGE	11	14	Jean-Yves KOUE NIATE
Sean RAGGETT	25	15	Jordan FAGBOLA
Tom CHAMPION	26	19	Harry WHITE
Nathan ARNOLD	28	20	Jamey OSBORNE
Alex WOODYARD	30	22	Omari STERLING-JAMES
subs		*subs*	
Jack MULDOON	7	8	Jack BYRNE
Alan POWER	8	9	Andy BROWN
Harry ANDERSON	12	17	Stefan MOORE
Lee BEEVERS	18	24	Lewis HAYDEN
Macauley BONNE	29	1	Danny LEWIS

REFEREE: Tom Nield
ASSISTANTS: Matthew Smith & Abbas Khan
FOURTH OFFICIAL: Scott Postin
ATTENDANCE: 4,049 (22 visiting supporters)

TEAM	P	W	D	L	F	A	GD	PTS
1. LINCOLN CITY	**10**	**7**	**1**	**2**	**22**	**8**	**14**	**22**
2. Dag & Red	10	7	0	3	19	9	10	21
3. Forest Green	10	6	2	2	20	11	9	20
4. Tranmere	10	6	2	2	12	7	5	20
5. Macclesfield	9	6	0	3	16	10	6	18
6. Aldershot	10	5	3	2	13	8	5	18
7. Barrow	10	5	3	2	15	12	3	18
8. Gateshead	10	5	1	4	20	11	9	16
9. Eastleigh	10	4	4	2	17	10	7	16
10. Dover	10	5	1	4	17	16	1	16
11. Wrexham	9	4	3	2	9	10	-1	15
12. Boreham Wood	10	3	5	2	12	8	4	14
13. Maidstone United	10	4	2	4	13	14	-1	14
14. Sutton United	10	4	1	5	11	13	-2	13
15. Torquay	10	4	1	5	11	13	-2	13
16. York	10	3	3	4	14	15	-1	12
17. Chester	10	3	2	5	15	15	0	11
18. Bromley	10	3	2	5	12	16	-4	11
19. SOLIHULL MOORS	**10**	**3**	**2**	**5**	**13**	**20**	**-7**	**11**
20. North Ferriby	10	3	1	6	6	17	-11	10
21. Braintree	10	2	3	5	10	16	-6	9
22. Woking	10	2	2	6	14	21	-7	8
23. Southport	10	1	2	7	7	26	-19	5
24. Guiseley	10	0	2	8	9	21	-12	2

KEY POINTS: Debut for Tom Champion

LINCOLN CITY 1
BARROW 2

Sincil Bank Stadium | 17.09.16

LINCOLN CITY		BARROW	
Paul FARMAN	1	1	Joel DIXON
Bradley WOOD	2	3	Nick ANDERTON
Sam HABERGHAM	3	5	Danny LIVESEY
Luke WATERFALL	5	6	Moussa DIARRA
Matt RHEAD	9	8	Alex-Ray HARVEY
Harry ANDERSON	12	9	Richard BENNETT
Sean RAGGETT	25	11	Jordan WILLIAMS
Tom CHAMPION	26	18	Liam HUGHES
Nathan ARNOLD	28	20	Byron HARRISON
Macauley BONNE	29	21	Dominic SMITH
Alex WOODYARD	30	22	Ryan YATES
subs		subs	
Jack MULDOON	7	7	Andy HAWORTH
Alan POWER	8	10	Ross HANNAH
Adam MARRIOTT	10	16	Lindon MEIKLE
Terry HAWKRIDGE	11	17	Paul TURNBULL
Lee BEEVERS	18	19	Euan MURRAY

REFEREE: Anthony Serrano
ASSISTANTS: Tom Hancock & Rob Evans
FOURTH OFFICIAL: Richie Watkins
ATTENDANCE: 3,578 (102 visiting supporters)

TEAM	P	W	D	L	F	A	GD	PTS
1. Dag & Red	11	8	0	3	21	9	12	24
2. Forest Green	11	7	2	2	21	11	10	23
3. LINCOLN CITY	**11**	**7**	**1**	**3**	**23**	**10**	**13**	**22**
4. BARROW	**11**	**6**	**3**	**2**	**17**	**13**	**4**	**21**
5. Tranmere	11	6	2	3	12	8	4	20
6. Eastleigh	11	5	4	2	18	10	8	19
7. Aldershot	11	5	4	2	14	9	5	19
8. Dover	11	6	1	4	18	16	2	19
9. Macclesfield	10	6	0	4	16	11	5	18
10. Gateshead	11	5	2	4	20	11	9	17
11. Boreham Wood	11	4	5	2	14	8	6	17
12. Sutton United	11	5	1	5	12	13	-1	16
13. Maidstone United	11	4	3	4	14	15	-1	15
14. Wrexham	10	4	3	3	9	12	-3	15
15. Chester	11	4	2	5	16	15	1	14
16. Torquay	11	4	1	6	11	15	-4	13
17. York	11	3	3	5	14	16	-2	12
18. Solihull Moors	11	3	3	5	13	20	-7	12
19. Woking	11	3	2	6	16	21	-5	11
20. Bromley	11	3	2	6	12	17	-5	11
21. North Ferriby	11	3	1	7	6	19	-13	10
22. Braintree	11	2	3	6	10	17	-7	9
23. Southport	11	1	3	7	8	27	-19	6
24. Guiseley	11	0	3	8	10	22	-12	3

33

DOVER ATHLETIC 2
LINCOLN CITY 0

Crabble, Lewisham Road | 24.09.16

DOVER ATHLETIC			LINCOLN CITY
Steve ARNOLD	18	1	Paul FARMAN
Sam MAGRI	2	2	Bradley WOOD
Aswad THOMAS	3	3	Sam HABERGHAM
Jim STEVENSON	8	5	Luke WATERFALL
Ricky MILLER	9	7	Jack MULDOON
Jamie GRIMES	15	9	Matt RHEAD
Tyrone STERLING	16	25	Sean RAGGETT
Moses EMMANUEL	17	26	Tom CHAMPION
Sammy MOORE	21	28	Nathan ARNOLD
Jack PARKINSON	23	29	Macauley BONNE
Ross LAFAYETTE	25	30	Alex WOODYARD
subs			*subs*
Chris KINNEAR	4	8	Alan POWER
Ayo OBILEYE	5	10	Adam MARRIOTT
Mitchell PINNOCK	11	11	Terry HAWKRIDGE
Loui FAZAKERLEY	12	12	Harry ANDERSON
Ira JACKSON	19	18	Lee BEEVERS

REFEREE: David Rock
ASSISTANTS: Kieran Bailey & Paul Saunders
FOURTH OFFICIAL: Oliver Jackson
ATTENDANCE: 1,209 (150 City supporters)

TEAM	P	W	D	L	F	A	GD	PTS
1. Dag & Red	12	9	0	3	24	10	14	27
2. Forest Green	12	8	2	2	22	11	11	26
3. Barrow	12	7	3	2	19	13	6	24
4. Tranmere	12	7	2	3	15	9	6	23
5. LINCOLN CITY	**12**	**7**	**1**	**4**	**23**	**12**	**11**	**22**
6. Eastleigh	12	6	4	2	20	11	9	22
7. Aldershot	12	6	4	2	17	9	8	22
8. DOVER	**12**	**7**	**1**	**4**	**20**	**16**	**4**	**22**
9. Macclesfield	11	7	0	4	18	12	6	21
10. Boreham Wood	12	4	6	2	15	9	6	18
11. Maidstone United	12	5	3	4	17	17	0	18
12. Gateshead	12	5	2	5	20	14	6	17
13. Sutton United	12	5	1	6	13	15	-2	16
14. Wrexham	11	4	4	3	9	12	-3	16
15. Chester	12	4	3	5	16	15	1	15
16. Torquay	12	4	1	7	13	18	-5	13
17. Solihull Moors	12	3	4	5	14	21	-7	13
18. York	12	3	3	6	14	18	-4	12
19. Woking	12	3	2	7	17	24	-7	11
20. Bromley	12	3	2	7	13	20	-7	11
21. North Ferriby	12	3	1	8	6	20	-14	10
22. Braintree	12	2	3	7	10	18	-8	9
23. Southport	12	2	3	7	9	27	-18	9
24. Guiseley	12	0	3	9	11	24	-13	3

Grimes

Beevers for Raggett

Emmanuel

Marriott for Rhead
Champion

Sterling

Pinnock for Emmanuel
Anderson for Muldoon

LINCOLN CITY 3
BRAINTREE TOWN 0
Sincil Bank Stadium | 01.10.16

LINCOLN CITY		BRAINTREE TOWN	
Paul FARMAN	1	1	Will PUDDY
Bradley WOOD	2	3	Jerome OKIMO
Sam HABERGHAM	3	4	Harry LEE
Luke WATERFALL	5	6	Jon ASHTON
Matt RHEAD	9	7	Jack MIDSON
Terry HAWKRIDGE	11	8	Chez ISAAC
Lee BEEVERS	18	10	Simeon AKINOLA
Sean RAGGETT	25	11	Craig BRAHAM-BARRETT
Nathan ARNOLD	28	14	Ollie MULDOON
Macauley BONNE	29	18	Jake GOODMAN
Alex WOODYARD	30	23	Michael CHEEK
subs		*subs*	
Jack MULDOON	7	2	Barney WILLIAMS
Alan POWER	8	9	Lee BARNARD
Harry ANDERSON	12	16	Brandon GOODSHIP
Tom CHAMPION	26	19	Jack COWGILL
Jamie McCOMBE	27	20	Sam CORNE

REFEREE: Steve Rushton
ASSISTANTS: Mark Cunliffe & Richard Woodward
FOURTH OFFICIAL: Andrew Dallison
ATTENDANCE: 3,554 (66 visiting supporters)

TEAM	P	W	D	L	F	A	GD	PTS
1. Dag & Red	13	9	1	3	24	10	14	28
2. Forest Green	13	8	3	2	22	11	11	27
3. Macclesfield	13	9	0	4	22	12	10	27
4. LINCOLN CITY	**13**	**8**	**1**	**4**	**26**	**12**	**14**	**25**
5. Aldershot	13	7	4	2	18	9	9	25
6. Barrow	13	7	4	2	19	13	6	25
7. Tranmere	13	7	3	3	15	9	6	24
8. Eastleigh	13	6	5	2	23	14	9	23
9. Dover	13	7	1	5	20	21	-1	22
10. Sutton United	13	6	1	6	14	15	-1	19
11. Wrexham	13	5	4	4	10	15	-5	19
12. Chester	13	5	3	5	21	15	6	18
13. Gateshead	13	5	3	5	20	14	6	18
14. Boreham Wood	13	4	6	3	15	10	5	18
15. Maidstone United	13	5	3	5	19	21	-2	18
16. Solihull Moors	13	4	4	5	18	23	-5	16
17. Torquay	13	4	2	7	13	18	-5	14
18. Bromley	13	4	2	7	15	21	-6	14
19. York	13	3	3	7	14	19	-5	12
20. Woking	13	3	3	7	20	27	-7	12
21. North Ferriby	13	3	1	9	6	21	-15	10
22. BRAINTREE	**13**	**2**	**3**	**8**	**10**	**21**	**-11**	**9**
23. Southport	13	2	3	8	10	29	-19	9
24. Guiseley	13	0	3	10	11	25	-14	3

Arnold | Cowgill for Ashton | Williams for Goodman | Waterfall | Muldoon for Rhead / Anderson for Hawkridge / Barnard for Muldoon | Williams | Muldoon

WREXHAM 1
LINCOLN CITY 2
Racecourse Ground | 04.10.16

WREXHAM			LINCOLN CITY
Shwan JALAL	1	1	Paul FARMAN
Hamza BENCHERIF	4	2	Bradley WOOD
Curtis TILT	6	3	Sam HABERGHAM
John ROONEY	10	5	Luke WATERFALL
Sean NEWTON	11	9	Matt RHEAD
Kai EDWARDS	12	12	Harry ANDERSON
Mark CARRINGTON	13	18	Lee BEEVERS
Paul RUTHERFORD	14	25	Sean RAGGETT
Rob EVANS	15	28	Nathan ARNOLD
Jordan EVANS	16	29	Macauley BONNE
Tyler HARVEY	29	30	Alex WOODYARD
subs			subs
Anthony BARRY	7	7	Jack MULDOON
Callum POWELL	17	8	Alan POWER
Shaun HARRAD	18	11	Terry HAWKRIDGE
Gerry McDONAGH	20	26	Tom CHAMPION
Nortei NORTEY	23	27	Jamie McCOMBE

REFEREE: Sam Allison
ASSISTANTS: Oliver Bickle & Michael Barlow
FOURTH OFFICIAL: Ian Hurdle
ATTENDANCE: 3,487 (137 City supporters)

TEAM	P	W	D	L	F	A	GD	PTS
1. Forest Green	14	9	3	2	26	11	15	30
2. LINCOLN CITY	**14**	**9**	**1**	**4**	**28**	**13**	**15**	**28**
3. Dag & Red	14	9	1	4	24	11	13	28
4. Macclesfield	14	9	1	4	23	13	10	28
5. Eastleigh	14	7	5	2	26	14	12	26
6. Barrow	14	7	5	2	20	14	6	26
7. Aldershot	14	7	4	3	18	13	5	25
8. Dover	14	8	1	5	23	22	1	25
9. Tranmere	14	7	3	4	15	10	5	24
10. Chester	14	6	3	5	22	15	7	21
11. Gateshead	14	6	3	5	21	14	7	21
12. Boreham Wood	14	5	6	3	17	11	6	21
13. Solihull Moors	14	5	4	5	22	23	-1	19
14. Sutton United	14	6	1	7	15	18	-3	19
15. WREXHAM	**14**	**5**	**4**	**5**	**11**	**17**	**-6**	**19**
16. Maidstone United	14	5	3	6	19	24	-5	18
17. Torquay	14	5	2	7	14	18	-4	17
18. Bromley	14	5	2	7	17	22	-5	17
19. Woking	14	3	3	8	21	29	-8	12
20. York	14	3	3	8	15	25	-10	12
21. North Ferriby	14	3	1	10	6	22	-16	10
22. Braintree	14	2	3	9	11	23	-12	9
23. Southport	14	2	3	9	10	33	-23	9
24. Guiseley	14	1	3	10	17	26	-9	6

KEY POINTS: Sub debut for Theo Robinson

BROMLEY 1
LINCOLN CITY 1

Hayes Lane | 08.10.16

BROMLEY			LINCOLN CITY
Alan JULIAN	1	1	Paul FARMAN
Joe HOWE	2	2	Bradley WOOD
Daniel JOHNSON	3	3	Sam HABERGHAM
Rob SWAINE	5	5	Luke WATERFALL
David MARTIN	7	7	Jack MULDOON
Adam CUNNINGTON	10	9	Matt RHEAD
Joe ANDERSON	13	12	Harry ANDERSON
Jordan HIGGS	14	18	Lee BEEVERS
Reece PRESTEDGE	16	25	Sean RAGGETT
Blair TURGOTT	17	28	Nathan ARNOLD
Oluwatobi SHO-SILVA	20	30	Alex WOODYARD
subs			*subs*
Jack HOLLAND	6	8	Alan POWER
Lee MINSHULL	8	11	Terry HAWKRIDGE
Connor DYMOND	12	26	Tom CHAMPION
Max HUXTER	23	29	Macauley BONNE
Daniel AJAKAIYE	24	31	Theo ROBINSON

REFEREE: Anthony Serrano
ASSISTANTS: Michael Ryan & Paul Lister
FOURTH OFFICIAL: Stuart Franklin
ATTENDANCE: 1,511 (304 City supporters)

TEAM	P	W	D	L	F	A	GD	PTS
1. Forest Green	15	10	3	2	29	11	18	33
2. Dag & Red	15	10	1	4	25	11	14	31
3. LINCOLN CITY	**15**	**9**	**2**	**4**	**29**	**14**	**15**	**29**
4. Barrow	15	8	5	2	23	14	9	29
5. Macclesfield	15	9	1	5	23	15	8	28
6. Aldershot	15	8	4	3	20	13	7	28
7. Tranmere	15	8	3	4	17	10	7	27
8. Eastleigh	15	7	5	3	26	15	11	26
9. Dover	15	8	1	6	25	26	-1	25
10. Gateshead	15	7	3	5	25	16	9	24
11. Chester	15	7	3	5	23	15	8	24
12. Boreham Wood	15	6	6	3	19	11	8	24
13. Sutton United	15	7	1	7	19	19	0	22
14. Solihull Moors	15	5	4	6	22	25	-3	19
15. Wrexham	15	5	4	6	11	19	-8	19
16. BROMLEY	**15**	**5**	**3**	**7**	**18**	**23**	**-5**	**18**
17. Maidstone United	15	5	3	7	19	27	-8	18
18. Torquay	15	5	2	8	14	19	-5	17
19. York	15	3	4	8	16	26	-10	13
20. Woking	15	3	3	9	22	33	-11	12
21. Braintree	15	2	4	9	12	24	-12	10
22. North Ferriby	15	3	1	11	6	25	-19	10
23. Guiseley	15	2	3	10	19	27	-8	9
24. Southport	15	2	3	10	11	35	-24	9

Sho-Silva · Cunnington · Swaine · Muldoon · Raggett — Anderson — Woodyard Minshull for Prestedge · Champion for Arnold — Turgott · Bonne for Rhead · Ajakaiye for Martin · Habergham — Robinson for Wood · Higgs · Holland for Cunnington

LINCOLN CITY 0
GUISELEY 0

Emirates FA Cup Fourth Round Qualifying
Sincil Bank Stadium | 15.10.16

LINCOLN CITY			GUISELEY
Paul FARMAN	1	17	Dan ATKINSON
Bradley WOOD	2	2	Connor BROWN
Sam HABERGHAM	3	3	Danny LOWE
Luke WATERFALL	5	6	Jake LAWLOR
Jack MULDOON	7	8	Will HATFIELD
Matt RHEAD	9	19	Jordan PRESTON
Terry HAWKRIDGE	11	22	Alex PURVER
Harry ANDERSON	12	24	Simon WALTON
Lee BEEVERS	18	25	Rob ATKINSON
Sean RAGGETT	25	29	Jake CASSIDY
Alex WOODYARD	30	30	Jermaine HYLTON
subs		subs	
Alan POWER	8	9	Adam BOYES
Jack FIXTER	22	10	Oli JOHNSON
Jack McMENEMY	24	11	Michael RANKINE
Jamie McCOMBE	27	15	Ash PALMER
Theo ROBINSON	31	18	Nicky CLEE
Luke ANDERSEN	32	20	Marcus WILLIAMS
Jimmy WALKER	23	12	Steve DICKINSON

REFEREE: Karl Evans
ASSISTANTS: Sean Feerick & Jonathan Burridge
FOURTH OFFICIAL: Harry Hawkins
ATTENDANCE: 2,629 (80 visiting supporters)

KEY POINTS: First time on teamsheet for Jack Fixter, Jack McMenemy & Luke Anderson (all scholars) | Assistant Referee Sean Feerick was replaced at half-time by Harry Hawkins due to injury | Andrew Doughty took over as Fourth Official

R Atkinson

Rankine for Hylton
Robinson for Muldoon

Wood

Johnson for Preston

Power for Wood

1 2 3 4 5 6 7 8 9 10 11 12 13 14 15 16 17 18 19 20 21 22 23 24 25 26 27 28 29 30 31 32 33 34 35 36 37 38 39 40 41 42 43 44 45 46 47 48 49 50 51 52 53 54 55 56 57 58 59 60 61 62 63 64 65 66 67 68 69 70 71 72 73 74 75 76 77 78 79 80 81 82 83 84 85 86 87 88 89 90

GUISELEY 1
LINCOLN CITY 2

Emirates FA Cup Fourth Round Qualifying Replay
Nethermoor Park | 17.10.16

GUISELEY			LINCOLN CITY
Dan ATKINSON	17	1	Paul FARMAN
Connor BROWN	2	2	Bradley WOOD
Jake LAWLOR	6	3	Sam HABERGHAM
Will HATFIELD	8	5	Luke WATERFALL
Adam BOYES	9	9	Matt RHEAD
Michael RANKINE	11	11	Terry HAWKRIDGE
Nicky CLEE	18	12	Harry ANDERSON
Marcus WILLIAMS	20	18	Lee BEEVERS
Alex PURVER	22	25	Sean RAGGETT
Simon WALTON	24	30	Alex WOODYARD
Rob ATKINSON	25	31	Theo ROBINSON
subs		*subs*	
Danny LOWE	3	7	Jack MULDOON
Oli JOHNSON	10	8	Alan POWER
Steve DICKINSON	12	22	Jack FIXTER
Ash PALMER	15	24	Jack McMENEMY
Jordan PRESTON	19	27	Jamie McCOMBE
Jake CASSIDY	29	32	Luke ANDERSEN
Jermaine HYLTON	30	23	Jimmy WALKER

REFEREE: Andrew Miller
ASSISTANTS: Paul Brown & John Matthews
FOURTH OFFICIAL: Bradley Hall
ATTENDANCE: 765 (177 City supporters)

KEY POINTS: Full debut for Theo Robinson | First LCFC goal for Theo Robinson

Robinson

Robinson
Walton

Boyes

Brown

Muldoon for Rhead

Hylton for Walton · Power for Robinson

Preston for Hatfield · Cassidy for Rankine

LINCOLN CITY 0
EASTLEIGH 0

Sincil Bank Stadium | 22.10.16

LINCOLN CITY		EASTLEIGH	
Paul FARMAN	1	13	Ryan HUDDART
Bradley WOOD	2	2	Joe PARTINGTON
Sam HABERGHAM	3	3	Michael GREEN
Luke WATERFALL	5	8	Andy DRURY
Matt RHEAD	9	10	Jai REASON
Harry ANDERSON	12	15	Luke COULSON
Lee BEEVERS	18	19	Mikael MANDRON
Sean RAGGETT	25	25	Ryan CRESSWELL
Nathan ARNOLD	28	26	Ryan BIRD
Alex WOODYARD	30	27	Reda JOHNSON
Theo ROBINSON	31	28	Jason TAYLOR
subs		*subs*	
Elliott WHITEHOUSE	4	6	David PIPE
Jack MULDOON	7	9	James CONSTABLE
Alan POWER	8	12	Jake HOWELL
Terry HAWKRIDGE	11	17	Adam DAWSON
Jamie McCOMBE	27	30	Jamie CURETON

REFEREE: Tom Nield
ASSISTANTS: Alex Guy & Martyn Holmes
FOURTH OFFICIAL: Hallam Cutmore
ATTENDANCE: 3,180 (74 visiting supporters)

TEAM	P	W	D	L	F	A	GD	PTS
1. Forest Green	16	11	3	2	32	11	21	36
2. Dag & Red	16	10	2	4	26	12	14	32
3. LINCOLN CITY	**16**	**9**	**3**	**4**	**29**	**14**	**15**	**30**
4. Tranmere	16	9	3	4	20	10	10	30
5. Barrow	16	8	6	2	24	15	9	30
6. Macclesfield	16	9	2	5	24	16	8	29
7. Aldershot	16	8	5	3	20	13	7	29
8. Dover	16	9	1	6	31	27	4	28
9. Gateshead	16	8	3	5	27	16	11	27
10. EASTLEIGH	**16**	**7**	**6**	**3**	**26**	**15**	**11**	**27**
11. Boreham Wood	16	7	6	3	20	11	9	27
12. Chester	16	7	4	5	24	16	8	25
13. Sutton United	16	7	2	7	20	20	0	23
14. Wrexham	16	6	4	6	13	20	-7	22
15. Solihull Moors	16	5	4	7	22	28	-6	19
16. Torquay	16	5	3	8	14	19	-5	18
17. Bromley	16	5	3	8	19	25	-6	18
18. Maidstone United	16	5	3	8	19	29	-10	18
19. York	16	3	5	8	17	27	-10	14
20. Woking	16	3	4	9	23	34	-11	13
21. Braintree	16	2	4	10	13	30	-17	10
22. North Ferriby	16	3	1	12	6	26	-20	10
23. Southport	16	2	4	10	12	36	-24	10
24. Guiseley	16	2	3	11	19	30	-11	9

Whitehouse for Rhead
Howell for Mandron
Muldoon for Anderson
Taylor
Constable for Bird
Raggett

KEY POINTS: Sub debut for Elliott Whitehouse

LINCOLN CITY 2
BOREHAM WOOD 0

Sincil Bank Stadium | 25.10.16

LINCOLN CITY		BOREHAM WOOD	
Paul FARMAN	1	1	Grant SMITH
Bradley WOOD	2	3	Danny WOODARDS
Sam HABERGHAM	3	4	Mark RICKETTS
Luke WATERFALL	5	5	Matt PAINE
Matt RHEAD	9	7	Ricky SHAKES
Harry ANDERSON	12	8	Kenny DAVIS
Lee BEEVERS	18	11	Bruno ANDRADE
Sean RAGGETT	25	15	Femi ILESANMI
Nathan ARNOLD	28	16	Conor CLIFFORD
Alex WOODYARD	30	19	Angelo BALANTA
Theo ROBINSON	31	33	Joe DEVERA
subs		*subs*	
Elliott WHITEHOUSE	4	2	Ben NUNN
Jack MULDOON	7	9	Jamie LUCAS
Alan POWER	8	14	Anthony JEFFREY
Terry HAWKRIDGE	11	20	Daniel UCHECHI
Jamie McCOMBE	27	23	Aaron KUHL

REFEREE: Tom Bramall
ASSISTANTS: Peter Sporne & Hristo Karaivanov
FOURTH OFFICIAL: David Hunt
ATTENDANCE: 3,014 (30 visiting supporters)

TEAM	P	W	D	L	F	A	GD	PTS
1. Forest Green	17	12	3	2	33	11	22	39
2. Dag & Red	17	11	2	4	27	12	15	35
3. LINCOLN CITY	**17**	**10**	**3**	**4**	**31**	**14**	**17**	**33**
4. Tranmere	17	10	3	4	21	10	11	33
5. Barrow	17	8	7	2	26	17	9	31
6. Dover	17	10	1	6	33	27	6	31
7. Eastleigh	17	8	6	3	29	15	14	30
8. Macclesfield	17	9	3	5	24	16	8	30
9. Aldershot	17	8	5	4	20	14	6	29
10. Gateshead	17	8	4	5	28	17	11	28
11. BOREHAM WOOD	**17**	**7**	**6**	**4**	**20**	**13**	**7**	**27**
12. Chester	17	7	5	5	24	16	8	26
13. Sutton United	17	7	3	7	22	22	0	24
14. Wrexham	17	6	5	6	15	22	-7	23
15. Solihull Moors	17	5	4	8	22	29	-7	19
16. Maidstone United	17	5	4	8	21	31	-10	19
17. Bromley	17	5	3	9	19	27	-8	18
18. Torquay	17	5	3	9	14	22	-8	18
19. York	17	3	5	9	17	29	-12	14
20. Woking	17	3	4	10	25	37	-12	13
21. Braintree	17	3	4	10	16	32	-16	13
22. Southport	17	3	4	10	14	36	-22	13
23. Guiseley	17	2	4	11	20	31	-11	10
24. North Ferriby	17	3	1	13	6	27	-21	10

Power for Beevers

Arnold
Jeffrey for Shakes

Ricketts
Lucas for Davis

Rhead
Whitehouse for Rhead
Muldoon for Robinson
Kuhl for Ricketts
Raggett

1 2 3 4 5 6 7 8 9 10 11 12 13 14 15 16 17 18 19 20 21 22 23 24 25 26 27 28 29 30 31 32 33 34 35 36 37 38 39 40 41 42 43 44 45 46 47 48 49 50 51 52 53 54 55 56 57 58 59 60 61 62 63 64 65 66 67 68 69 70 71 72 73 74 75 76 77 78 79 80 81 82 83 84 85 86 87 88 89 90

KEY POINTS: Lee Beevers stretchered off | Boreham Wood goalkeeping coach sent to stands following an incident with Fourth Official

CHESTER 2
LINCOLN CITY 5
The Lookers Vauxhall Stadium | 29.10.16

CHESTER			LINCOLN CITY
Alex LYNCH	1	1	Paul FARMAN
Blaine HUDSON	5	2	Bradley WOOD
Sam HUGHES	12	3	Sam HABERGHAM
Ryan ASTLES	6	5	Luke WATERFALL
Johnny HUNT	16	8	Alan POWER
Tom SHAW	8	9	Matt RHEAD
Ryan LLOYD	21	12	Harry ANDERSON
Craig MAHON	7	25	Sean RAGGETT
Elliott DURRELL	10	28	Nathan ARNOLD
Jordan CHAPELL	11	30	Alex WOODYARD
James ALABI	9	31	Theo ROBINSON
subs		*subs*	
Evan HORWOOD	3	4	Elliott WHITEHOUSE
Wade JOYCE	14	7	Jack MULDOON
Kane RICHARDS	15	11	Terry HAWKRIDGE
James AKINTUNDE	20	14	Taylor MILES
Matty WATERS	19	27	Jamie McCOMBE

REFEREE: Anthony Backhouse
ASSISTANTS: Richard Watson & Mark Billingham
FOURTH OFFICIAL: Richard Woodward
ATTENDANCE: 2,586 (413 City supporters)

TEAM	P	W	D	L	F	A	GD	PTS
1. Forest Green	18	12	4	2	34	12	22	40
2. LINCOLN CITY	**18**	**11**	**3**	**4**	**36**	**16**	**20**	**36**
3. Dag & Red	18	11	3	4	28	13	15	36
4. Tranmere	18	11	3	4	25	11	14	36
5. Barrow	18	9	7	2	30	17	13	34
6. Aldershot	18	9	5	4	21	14	7	32
7. Dover	18	10	1	7	34	31	3	31
8. Eastleigh	18	8	6	4	29	19	10	30
9. Boreham Wood	18	8	6	4	22	14	8	30
10. Macclesfield	18	9	3	6	25	18	7	30
11. Gateshead	18	8	5	5	30	19	11	29
12. CHESTER	**18**	**7**	**5**	**6**	**26**	**21**	**5**	**26**
13. Sutton United	18	7	4	7	24	24	0	25
14. Wrexham	18	6	6	6	17	24	-7	24
15. Solihull Moors	18	6	4	8	23	29	-6	22
16. Maidstone United	18	6	4	8	23	32	-9	22
17. Bromley	18	6	3	9	21	28	-7	21
18. Torquay	18	5	3	10	15	24	-9	18
19. Southport	18	4	4	10	16	37	-21	16
20. York	18	3	6	9	19	31	-12	15
21. Woking	18	3	4	11	26	39	-13	13
22. Braintree	18	3	4	11	16	33	-17	13
23. Guiseley	18	2	4	12	20	32	-12	10
24. North Ferriby	18	3	1	14	7	29	-22	10

LINCOLN CITY 2
ALTRINCHAM 1

Emirates FA Cup Round One
Sincil Bank Stadium | 05.11.16

LINCOLN CITY				ALTRINCHAM
Paul FARMAN	1		1	Andrew DAWBER
Bradley WOOD	2		2	Curtis OBENG
Sam HABERGHAM	3		3	Andy McWILLIAMS
Luke WATERFALL	5		4	Jake MOULT
Alan POWER	8		5	John CYRUS
Matt RHEAD	9		6	Tom HANNIGAN
Harry ANDERSON	12		7	James LAWRIE
Sean RAGGETT	25		8	Simon LENIGHAN
Nathan ARNOLD	28		9	Greg WILKINSON
Alex WOODYARD	30		10	Damian REEVES
Theo ROBINSON	31		11	Sean MILLER
subs			subs	
Jack MULDOON	7		12	Phil MARSH
Adam MARRIOTT	10		14	Simon RICHMAN
Terry HAWKRIDGE	11		15	Sam HEATHCOTE
Taylor MILES	14		16	Sam PATTERSON
Jamie McCOMBE	27		17	Billy HASLER-CREGG
Jack WEATHERELL	29		18	Danny HALL
Richard WALTON	21		20	Tim DEASY

REFEREE: Steve Rushton
ASSISTANTS: Richard Watson & Mark Billingham
FOURTH OFFICIAL: Richard Woodward
ATTENDANCE: 3,529 (161 visiting supporters)

Raggett — McWilliams / Patterson for Hannigan — Muldoon for Robinson / Power — Richman for Lenighan / Marsh for Obeng — Wilkinson / Hawkridge for Rhead / Cyrus — Hawkridge

LINCOLN CITY 3
ALDERSHOT TOWN 3

Sincil Bank Stadium | 12.11.16

LINCOLN CITY		ALDERSHOT TOWN	
Paul FARMAN	1	1 Jake COLE	
Bradley WOOD	2	2 Nick ARNOLD	
Sam HABERGHAM	3	5 Will EVANS	
Luke WATERFALL	5	9 Scott RENDELL	
Alan POWER	8	10 Matt McCLURE	
Matt RHEAD	9	11 Bernard MENSAH	
Harry ANDERSON	12	12 Cheye ALEXANDER	
Sean RAGGETT	25	16 Jake GALLAGHER	
Nathan ARNOLD	28	18 Dion CONROY	
Alex WOODYARD	30	19 Idris KANU	
Theo ROBINSON	31	22 Callum REYNOLDS	
subs		*subs*	
Elliott WHITEHOUSE	4	3 Anthony STRAKER	
Jack MULDOON	7	6 Jack SAVILLE	
Adam MARRIOTT	10	8 Charlie WALKER	
Terry HAWKRIDGE	11	17 Jim KELLERMANN	
Jamie McCOMBE	27	25 Mark SMITH	

REFEREE: Martin Coy
ASSISTANTS: Paul Evans & Tom Hancock
FOURTH OFFICIAL: Wayne Chalmers
ATTENDANCE: 3,461 (159 visiting supporters)

TEAM	P	W	D	L	F	A	GD	PTS
1. Forest Green	20	14	4	2	37	13	24	46
2. LINCOLN CITY	**19**	**11**	**4**	**4**	**39**	**19**	**20**	**37**
3. Tranmere	19	11	4	4	27	13	14	37
4. Dag & Red	19	11	3	5	28	18	10	36
5. Barrow	19	9	8	2	30	17	13	35
6. Dover	19	11	1	7	37	33	4	34
7. ALDERSHOT	**20**	**9**	**6**	**5**	**25**	**19**	**6**	**33**
8. Gateshead	19	9	5	5	35	19	16	32
9. Eastleigh	19	8	7	4	30	20	10	31
10. Boreham Wood	19	8	6	5	22	15	7	30
11. Macclesfield	19	9	3	7	25	19	6	30
12. Chester	19	7	6	6	28	23	5	27
13. Sutton United	19	7	5	7	24	24	0	26
14. Wrexham	20	6	7	7	17	25	-8	25
15. Bromley	19	7	3	9	22	28	-6	24
16. Solihull Moors	19	6	4	9	25	32	-7	22
17. Maidstone United	19	6	4	9	25	35	-10	22
18. Southport	19	5	4	10	19	39	-20	19
19. Torquay	19	5	3	11	15	26	-11	18
20. York	19	3	7	9	20	32	-12	16
21. Braintree	19	4	4	11	17	33	-16	16
22. Woking	19	3	5	11	27	40	-13	14
23. Guiseley	19	3	4	12	22	32	-10	13
24. North Ferriby	20	3	3	14	8	30	-22	12

Kanu

Arnold
Arnold

Reynolds
Arnold

Muldoon for Anderson
Alexander

Rhead

Hawkridge for Arnold

Rendell
Whitehouse for Power

Raggett

Kellerman for McClure
Conroy
Rhead
Saville for Kanu

KEY POINTS: Lee Beevers stretchered off | Boreham Wood goalkeeping coach sent to stands following an incident with Fourth Official

KEY POINTS: Game shown live on BT Sport | Kick-off time 12.15pm | Alex Woodyard's first LCFC goal

FOREST GREEN ROVERS 2
LINCOLN CITY 3
The New Lawn | 19.11.16

FOREST GREEN ROVERS		LINCOLN CITY	
Sam RUSSELL	23	1	Paul FARMAN
Charlie CLOUGH	5	2	Bradley WOOD
Keanu MARSH-BROWN	7	3	Sam HABERGHAM
Christian DOIDGE	9	5	Luke WATERFALL
Elliott FREAR	11	8	Alan POWER
Darren CARTER	12	9	Matt RHEAD
Liam NOBLE	15	12	Harry ANDERSON
Ethan PINNOCK	16	25	Sean RAGGETT
Daniel WISHART	17	28	Nathan ARNOLD
Rob SINCLAIR	19	30	Alex WOODYARD
Aarran RACINE	21	31	Theo ROBINSON
subs		subs	
Drissa TRAORE	4	4	Elliott WHITEHOUSE
Dale BENNETT	6	7	Jack MULDOON
Marcus KELLY	10	10	Adam MARRIOTT
Matt TUBBS	20	11	Terry HAWKRIDGE
Rhys MURPHY	39	27	Jamie McCOMBE

REFEREE: Constantine Hatzidakis
ASSISTANTS: Simon Shaw & Grant Taylor
FOURTH OFFICIAL: Ian Rathbone
ATTENDANCE: 2,164 (345 City supporters)

TEAM	P	W	D	L	F	A	GD	PTS
1. FOREST GREEN	21	14	4	3	39	16	23	46
2. LINCOLN CITY	20	12	4	4	42	21	21	40
3. Tranmere	20	12	4	4	28	13	15	40
4. Dag & Red	20	12	3	5	30	18	12	39
5. Barrow	20	10	8	2	32	18	14	38
6. Dover	20	12	1	7	39	33	6	37
7. Gateshead	20	9	6	5	37	21	16	33
8. Boreham Wood	20	9	6	5	24	15	9	33
9. Macclesfield	20	10	3	7	27	20	7	33
10. Aldershot	21	9	6	6	26	21	5	33
11. Eastleigh	20	8	8	4	32	22	10	32
12. Chester	20	7	6	6	29	24	5	27
13. Sutton United	20	7	5	8	25	26	-1	26
14. Wrexham	21	6	8	7	18	26	-8	26
15. Bromley	20	7	4	9	23	29	-6	25
16. Solihull Moors	20	6	4	10	26	34	-8	22
17. Maidstone United	20	6	4	10	25	38	-13	22
18. Torquay	20	5	4	11	16	27	-11	19
19. Southport	20	5	4	11	19	41	-22	19
20. Woking	20	4	5	11	29	39	-10	17
21. York	20	3	7	10	20	34	-14	16
22. Braintree	20	4	4	12	17	34	-17	16
23. North Ferriby	21	4	3	14	9	30	-21	15
24. Guiseley	20	3	4	13	22	34	-12	13

KEY POINTS: Full debut for Elliott Whitehouse | First LCFC goal for Elliott Whitehouse

YORK CITY 1
LINCOLN CITY 4
Bootham Crescent | 22.11.16

YORK CITY			LINCOLN CITY
Scott FLINDERS	1	1	Paul FARMAN
Shaun ROONEY	2	2	Bradley WOOD
Matt FRY	6	3	Sam HABERGHAM
Simon HESLOP	8	4	Elliott WHITEHOUSE
Yan LUKOWSKI	10	5	Luke WATERFALL
Aidan CONNOLLY	12	6	Callum HOWE
Simon LAPPIN	19	9	Matt RHEAD
Charlie COOPER	31	11	Terry HAWKRIDGE
Robbie McDAID	32	28	Nathan ARNOLD
Sean NEWTON	33	30	Alex WOODYARD
Danny HOLMES	35	31	Theo ROBINSON
subs			*subs*
Alex WHITTLE	3	7	Jack MULDOON
Daniel NTI	7	8	Alan POWER
Scott FENWICK	21	10	Adam MARRIOTT
Matty DIXON	23	27	Jamie McCOMBE
Callum RZONCA	25	21	Richard WALTON

REFEREE: Tom Bramall
ASSISTANTS: Paul Brown & Rebecca Welch
FOURTH OFFICIAL: Chris Ellis
ATTENDANCE: 2,889 (1068 City supporters)

TEAM	P	W	D	L	F	A	GD	PTS
1. Forest Green	22	14	5	3	41	18	23	47
2. LINCOLN CITY	21	13	4	4	46	22	24	43
3. Dag & Red	21	13	3	5	31	18	13	42
4. Barrow	21	11	8	2	35	18	17	41
5. Tranmere	21	12	5	4	30	15	15	41
6. Dover	21	13	1	7	42	34	8	40
7. Boreham Wood	21	10	6	5	25	15	10	36
8. Eastleigh	21	9	8	4	33	22	11	35
9. Gateshead	21	9	7	5	38	22	16	34
10. Macclesfield	21	10	4	7	28	21	7	34
11. Aldershot	22	9	6	7	26	22	4	33
12. Chester	21	7	8	6	31	26	5	29
13. Sutton United	21	7	5	9	25	27	-2	26
14. Bromley	21	7	5	9	25	31	-6	26
15. Wrexham	21	6	8	7	18	26	-8	26
16. Torquay	21	6	4	11	19	27	-8	22
17. Solihull Moors	21	6	4	11	26	37	-11	22
18. Maidstone United	21	6	4	11	25	39	-14	22
19. Southport	21	5	5	11	21	43	-22	20
20. Woking	21	4	5	12	30	42	-12	17
21. Braintree	21	4	5	12	19	36	-17	17
22. YORK	21	3	7	11	21	38	-17	16
23. North Ferriby	21	4	3	14	9	30	-21	15
24. Guiseley	21	3	4	14	22	37	-15	13

Whitehouse
Klukowski
Arnold
Waterfall
Whittle for Fry
Nti for Connolly
Heslop
Rzonca for Cooper
Waterfall
Muldoon for Arnold
Klukowski
Power for Rhead
Wood
Marriott for Robinson
Hawkridge
Nti

LINCOLN CITY 2
MAIDSTONE UNITED 0

Sincil Bank Stadium | 26.11.16

LINCOLN CITY		MAIDSTONE UNITED	
Paul FARMAN	1	Lee WORGAN	1
Bradley WOOD	2	Tom MILLS	3
Sam HABERGHAM	3	Jamie COYLE	4
Luke WATERFALL	5	Kevin LOKKO	5
Alan POWER	8	James ROGERS	6
Matt RHEAD	9	Dan SWEENEY	8
Terry HAWKRIDGE	11	Jack PAXMAN	10
Sean RAGGETT	25	Bobby-Joe TAYLOR	16
Nathan ARNOLD	28	Seth Nana TWUMASI	22
Alex WOODYARD	30	Liam ENVER-MARUM	24
Theo ROBINSON	31	Jamar LOZA	25
subs		*subs*	
Elliott WHITEHOUSE	4	Callum DRIVER	2
Callum HOWE	6	Bradley HUDSON-ODOI	9
Jack MULDOON	7	Jack EVANS	12
Adam MARRIOTT	10	Ben GREENHALGH	17
Harry ANDERSON	12	Yemi ODUBADE	23

REFEREE: Wayne Barratt
ASSISTANTS: Jonathan Burridge & Martyn Holmes
FOURTH OFFICIAL: Steve Abbott
ATTENDANCE: 3,917 (208 visiting supporters)

TEAM	P	W	D	L	F	A	GD	PTS
1. Forest Green	23	14	5	4	42	21	21	47
2. LINCOLN CITY	**22**	**14**	**4**	**4**	**48**	**22**	**26**	**46**
3. Barrow	22	12	8	2	39	19	20	44
4. Tranmere	22	13	5	4	32	16	16	44
5. Dag & Red	22	13	3	6	32	22	10	42
6. Dover	21	13	1	7	42	34	8	40
7. Boreham Wood	22	10	6	6	26	18	8	36
8. Eastleigh	22	9	8	5	33	25	8	35
9. Gateshead	22	9	7	6	38	25	13	34
10. Macclesfield	21	10	4	7	28	21	7	34
11. Aldershot	23	9	6	8	26	24	2	33
12. Chester	22	8	8	6	34	26	8	32
13. Sutton United	22	8	5	9	27	27	0	29
14. Bromley	22	8	5	9	28	31	-3	29
15. Wrexham	22	7	8	7	21	27	-6	29
16. Solihull Moors	22	7	4	11	28	37	-9	25
17. Torquay	22	6	4	12	20	29	-9	22
18. MAIDSTONE	**22**	**6**	**4**	**12**	**25**	**41**	**-16**	**22**
19. Woking	22	5	5	12	34	43	-9	20
20. Braintree	22	5	5	12	24	40	-16	20
21. Southport	22	5	5	12	25	48	-23	20
22. Guiseley	22	4	4	14	25	38	-13	16
23. York	22	3	7	12	21	41	-20	16
24. North Ferriby	22	4	3	15	10	33	-23	15

Sweeney / Coyle
Robinson
Rhead
Hudson-Odoi for Sweeney
Muldoon for Arnold
Greenhalgh for Taylor / Odubade for Loza
Whitehouse for Rhead
Marriott for Robinson

LINCOLN CITY 1
WREXHAM 0

Sincil Bank Stadium | 29.11.16

LINCOLN CITY		WREXHAM	
Paul FARMAN	1	26	Luke CODDINGTON
Bradley WOOD	2	4	Hamza BENCHERIF
Sam HABERGHAM	3	6	Curtis TILT
Elliott WHITEHOUSE	4	10	John ROONEY
Luke WATERFALL	5	11	Rekeil PYKE
Matt RHEAD	9	12	Kai EDWARDS
Terry HAWKRIDGE	11	13	Mark CARRINGTON
Sean RAGGETT	25	14	Paul RUTHERFORD
Nathan ARNOLD	28	15	Rob EVANS
Alex WOODYARD	30	16	Jordan EVANS
Theo ROBINSON	31	20	Gerry McDONAGH
subs		subs	
Callum HOWE	6	5	Martin RILEY
Jack MULDOON	7	7	Anthony BARRY
Alan POWER	8	9	Jordan WHITE
Adam MARRIOTT	10	17	Callum POWELL
Harry ANDERSON	12	1	Shwan JALAL

REFEREE: David Rock
ASSISTANTS: Joshua Few & Andy Humphries
FOURTH OFFICIAL: Martin Chester
ATTENDANCE: 3,344 (75 visiting supporters)

TEAM	P	W	D	L	F	A	GD	PTS
1. LINCOLN CITY	**23**	**15**	**4**	**4**	**49**	**22**	**27**	**49**
2. Forest Green	23	14	5	4	42	21	21	47
3. Tranmere	23	14	5	4	33	16	17	47
4. Barrow	22	12	8	2	39	19	20	44
5. Dover	22	14	1	7	48	34	14	43
6. Dag & Red	23	13	3	7	32	23	9	42
7. Boreham Wood	22	10	6	6	26	18	8	36
8. Chester	23	9	8	6	37	26	11	35
9. Eastleigh	23	9	8	6	34	27	7	35
10. Gateshead	23	9	7	7	38	26	12	34
11. Macclesfield	21	10	4	7	28	21	7	34
12. Aldershot	23	9	6	8	26	24	2	33
13. Bromley	23	8	5	10	29	33	-4	29
14. Sutton United	23	8	5	10	27	33	-6	29
15. WREXHAM	**23**	**7**	**8**	**8**	**21**	**28**	**-7**	**29**
16. Solihull Moors	23	7	5	11	28	37	-9	26
17. Torquay	23	7	4	12	21	29	-8	25
18. Maidstone United	23	7	4	12	27	42	-15	25
19. Woking	23	6	5	12	36	44	-8	23
20. Southport	23	5	6	12	25	48	-23	21
21. Braintree	22	5	5	12	24	40	-16	20
22. Guiseley	23	4	5	14	26	39	-13	17
23. York	23	3	8	12	22	42	-20	17
24. North Ferriby	23	4	3	16	10	36	-26	15

KEY POINTS: Matt Rhead missed a 10th minute penalty

LINCOLN CITY 3
OLDHAM ATHLETIC 2

Emirates FA Cup Second Round
Sincil Bank Stadium | 05.12.16

LINCOLN CITY			OLDHAM ATHLETIC
Paul FARMAN	1	1	Connor RIPLEY
Bradley WOOD	2	3	Jamie RECKORD
Sam HABERGHAM	3	5	Cameron BURGESS
Luke WATERFALL	5	8	Oli BANKS
Alan POWER	8	10	Carl WINCHESTER
Matt RHEAD	9	12	Freddie LADAPO
Terry HAWKRIDGE	11	16	Cameron DUMMIGAN
Jamie McCOMBE	27	19	Lee ERWIN
Nathan ARNOLD	28	26	Peter CLARKE
Alex WOODYARD	30	27	Ryan McLAUGHLIN
Theo ROBINSON	31	28	Paul GREEN
subs			*subs*
Jack MULDOON	7	2	Josh LAW
Adam MARRIOTT	10	9	Billy McKAY
Harry ANDERSON	12	11	Lee CROFT
Jack FIXTER	22	18	Darius OSEI
Jack McMENEMY	24	24	Ousmane FANE
Jack WEATHERELL	29	31	Charles DUNNE
Richard WALTON	21	13	Chris KETTINGS

REFEREE: Gavin Ward
ASSISTANTS: James Bell & Nick Hopton
FOURTH OFFICIAL: Andy Madley
ATTENDANCE: 7,012 (415 visiting supporters)

KEY POINTS: Game shown live on BT Sport

LINCOLN CITY 2
TRANMERE ROVERS 1

Sincil Bank Stadium | 17.12.16

LINCOLN CITY		TRANMERE ROVERS	
Paul FARMAN	1	Scott DAVIES	1
Bradley WOOD	2	Lee VAUGHAN	2
Sam HABERGHAM	3	Liam RIDEHALGH	3
Elliott WHITEHOUSE	4	Steve McNULTY	5
Luke WATERFALL	5	Jay HARRIS	8
Callum HOWE	6	James NORWOOD	10
Matt RHEAD	9	Ritchie SUTTON	12
Terry HAWKRIDGE	11	Ben TOLLITT	18
Nathan ARNOLD	28	Andy MANGAN	19
Alex WOODYARD	30	Lois MAYNARD	20
Theo ROBINSON	31	Jeff HUGHES	24
subs		*subs*	
Jack MULDOON	7	Steven JENNINGS	4
Alan POWER	8	Michael IHIEKWE	6
Adam MARRIOTT	10	Jake KIRBY	17
Harry ANDERSON	12	James WALLACE	38
Jamie McCOMBE	27	Iain TURNER	13

REFEREE: Craig Hicks
ASSISTANTS: Abbas Khan & Paul Evans
FOURTH OFFICIAL: Wayne Porter
ATTENDANCE: 6,335 (807 visiting supporters)

TEAM	P	W	D	L	F	A	GD	PTS
1. LINCOLN CITY	**24**	**16**	**4**	**4**	**51**	**23**	**28**	**52**
2. TRANMERE	**25**	**15**	**5**	**5**	**35**	**18**	**17**	**50**
3. Forest Green	24	14	6	4	43	22	21	48
4. Dag & Red	25	14	4	7	38	28	10	46
5. Barrow	23	12	9	2	40	20	20	45
6. Dover	24	14	2	8	50	37	13	44
7. Chester	25	10	9	6	40	27	13	39
8. Macclesfield	23	11	4	8	32	23	9	37
9. Boreham Wood	24	10	7	7	27	21	6	37
10. Aldershot	25	10	6	9	28	26	2	36
11. Gateshead	25	9	8	8	39	28	11	35
12. Eastleigh	24	9	8	7	37	31	6	35
13. Bromley	25	10	5	10	33	34	-1	35
14. Sutton United	24	9	5	10	28	33	-5	32
15. Wrexham	25	7	8	10	21	32	-11	29
16. Solihull Moors	24	7	6	11	32	41	-9	27
17. Torquay	24	7	5	12	21	29	-8	26
18. Maidstone United	25	7	4	14	28	46	-18	25
19. Woking	24	6	6	12	36	44	-8	24
20. Southport	24	6	6	12	29	51	-22	24
21. Braintree	23	5	6	12	25	41	-16	21
22. North Ferriby	25	6	3	16	13	37	-24	21
23. Guiseley	24	4	7	14	27	40	-13	19
24. York	25	3	9	13	22	43	-21	18

Arnold

Hughes (pen)

Hawkridge

Anderson for Hawkridge

Kirby for Harris

Ridehalgh
Marriott for Robinson
Marriott

Rhead
McCombe for Rhead
Farman
Mangan

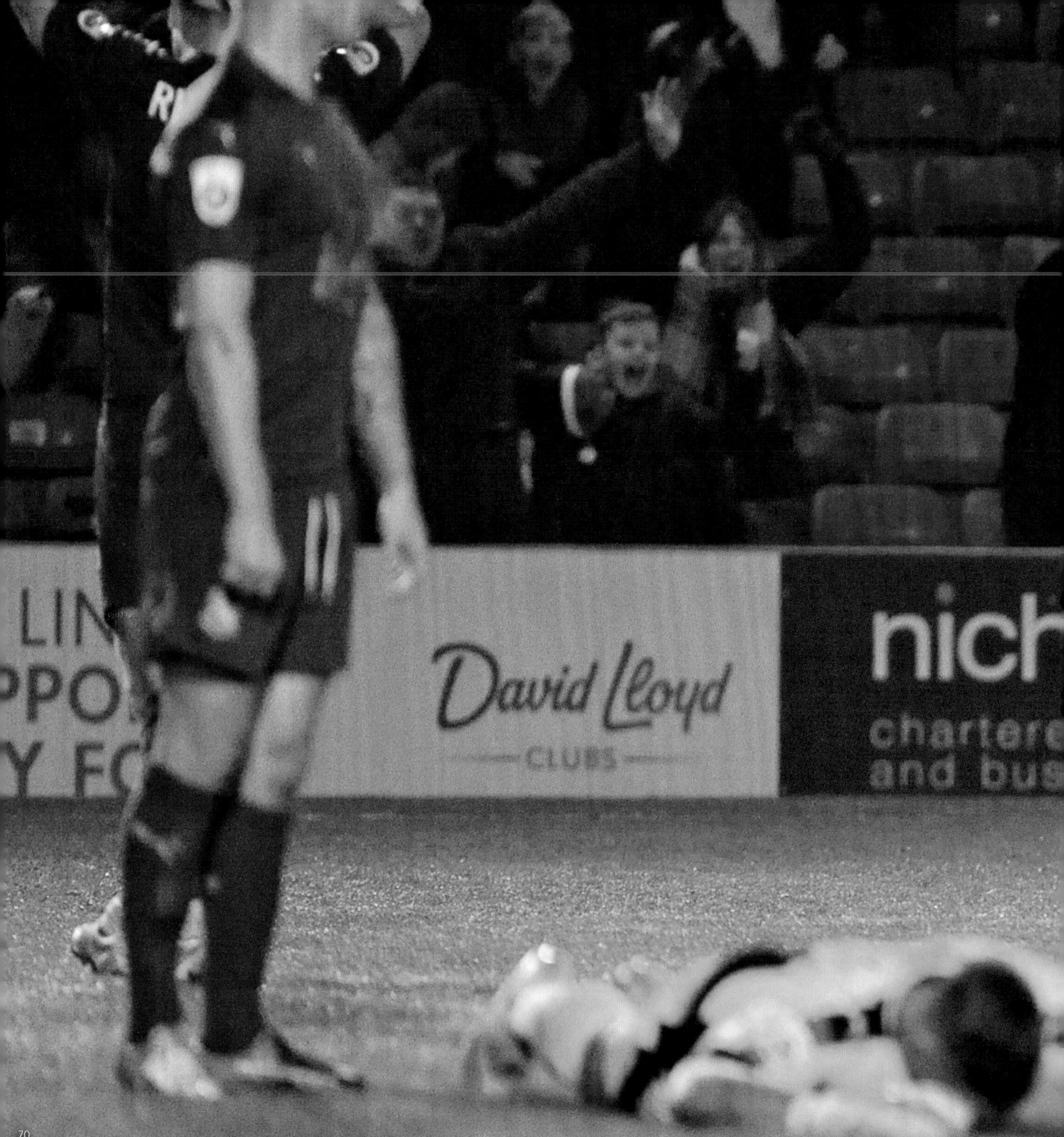
David Lloyd
CLUBS

KEY POINTS: LCFC's first ever game against Nantwich Town

NANTWICH TOWN 1
LINCOLN CITY 2

Buildbase FA Trophy First Round
Weaver Stadium | 20.12.16

NANTWICH TOWN			LINCOLN CITY
Dave PARTON	1	1	Paul FARMAN
Andy WHITE	2	2	Bradley WOOD
Ibou TOURAY	3	3	Sam HABERGHAM
Curtis JONES	4	4	Elliott WHITEHOUSE
Joel STAIR	5	6	Callum HOWE
Sam HALL	6	7	Jack MULDOON
Joe MWASILE	7	8	Alan POWER
Matt BELL	8	9	Matt RHEAD
Ryan BROOKE	9	10	Adam MARRIOTT
Oliver FINNEY	10	11	Terry HAWKRIDGE
Wayne RILEY	11	27	Jamie McCOMBE
subs		*subs*	
Osebi ABADAKI	12	5	Luke WATERFALL
Dave WALKER	14	28	Nathan ARNOLD
Steve JONES	15	30	Alex WOODYARD
Tim SANDERS	16	31	Theo ROBINSON
Reece QUINN	13	21	Richard WALTON

REFEREE: Scott Oldham
ASSISTANTS: Matt Pope & James Madine
FOURTH OFFICIAL: Lee Hible
ATTENDANCE: 482

Whitehouse

Arnold for Rhead Woodyard for Whitehouse

Hawkridge

Jones for Finney Abadaki for Mwasile

Walker for Brooke Robinson for Muldoon Farman (og)

GUISELEY 2
LINCOLN CITY 1

Nethermoor Park | 26.12.16

GUISELEY			LINCOLN CITY
Jonny MAXTED	26	1	Paul FARMAN
Connor BROWN	2	2	Bradley WOOD
Danny LOWE	3	3	Sam HABERGHAM
Will HATFIELD	8	4	Elliott WHITEHOUSE
Michael RANKINE	11	5	Luke WATERFALL
Ashley PALMER	15	9	Matt RHEAD
Jordan PRESTON	19	11	Terry HAWKRIDGE
Marcus WILLIAMS	20	25	Sean RAGGETT
Simon WALTON	24	28	Nathan ARNOLD
Jake CASSIDY	29	30	Alex WOODYARD
James WESOLOWSKI	31	31	Theo ROBINSON
subs			*subs*
Adam BOYES	9	6	Callum HOWE
Oli JOHNSON	10	7	Jack MULDOON
Dan ATKINSON	17	8	Alan POWER
Alex PURVER	22	10	Adam MARRIOTT
Elliott GREEN	33	14	Taylor MILES

REFEREE: Andrew Miller
ASSISTANTS: Oliver Bickle & Paul Lister
FOURTH OFFICIAL: Joe Starkie
ATTENDANCE: 2,446 (974 City supporters)

TEAM	P	W	D	L	F	A	GD	PTS
1. Tranmere	26	16	5	5	36	18	18	53
2. LINCOLN CITY	25	16	4	5	52	25	27	52
3. Forest Green	25	14	6	5	46	26	20	48
4. Barrow	24	12	10	2	40	20	20	46
5. Dag & Red	26	14	4	8	40	31	9	46
6. Dover	25	14	3	8	51	38	13	45
7. Chester	26	10	9	7	42	30	12	39
8. Aldershot	26	11	6	9	32	26	6	39
9. Bromley	26	11	5	10	34	34	0	38
10. Macclesfield	24	11	4	9	32	24	8	37
11. Boreham Wood	25	10	7	8	27	22	5	37
12. Gateshead	26	9	9	8	39	28	11	36
13. Eastleigh	24	9	8	7	37	31	6	35
14. Sutton United	25	9	5	11	28	34	-6	32
15. Wrexham	26	8	8	10	22	32	-10	32
16. Solihull Moors	25	8	6	11	35	43	-8	30
17. Torquay	25	8	5	12	25	32	-7	29
18. Braintree	25	7	6	12	29	43	-14	27
19. Maidstone United	26	7	5	14	29	47	-18	26
20. Woking	25	6	6	13	36	48	-12	24
21. Southport	25	6	6	13	29	52	-23	24
22. GUISELEY	26	5	7	14	29	41	-12	22
23. York	26	4	9	13	23	43	-20	21
24. North Ferriby	26	6	3	17	13	38	-25	21

LINCOLN CITY 3
GUISELEY 1

Sincil Bank Stadium | 01.01.17

LINCOLN CITY		GUISELEY	
Paul FARMAN	1	26	Jonny MAXTED
Bradley WOOD	2	2	Connor BROWN
Sam HABERGHAM	3	3	Danny LOWE
Luke WATERFALL	5	8	Will HATFIELD
Alan POWER	8	9	Adam BOYES
Matt RHEAD	9	15	Ashley PALMER
Terry HAWKRIDGE	11	19	Jordan PRESTON
Sean RAGGETT	25	20	Marcus WILLIAMS
Nathan ARNOLD	28	24	Simon WALTON
Alex WOODYARD	30	29	Jake CASSIDY
Theo ROBINSON	31	31	James WESOLOWSKI
subs		subs	
Callum HOWE	6	10	Oli JOHNSON
Jack MULDOON	7	22	Alex PURVER
Adam MARRIOTT	10	32	Joel LOGAN
Taylor MILES	14	33	Elliott GREEN
Richard WALTON	21	17	Dan ATKINSON

REFEREE: Chris O'Donnell
ASSISTANTS: Lee Freeman & Adam Burgess
FOURTH OFFICIAL: David Hunt
ATTENDANCE: 5,148 (101 visiting supporters)

TEAM	P	W	D	L	F	A	GD	PTS
1. LINCOLN CITY	**26**	**17**	**4**	**5**	**55**	**26**	**29**	**55**
2. Tranmere	27	16	5	6	38	22	16	53
3. Forest Green	26	14	7	5	51	31	20	49
4. Dover	26	15	3	8	55	39	16	48
5. Barrow	25	12	10	3	41	24	17	46
6. Dag & Red	26	14	4	8	40	31	9	46
7. Aldershot	27	12	6	9	34	27	7	42
8. Macclesfield	25	12	4	9	36	26	10	40
9. Gateshead	27	10	9	8	43	29	14	39
10. Chester	27	10	9	8	42	33	9	39
11. Eastleigh	26	10	9	7	40	33	7	39
12. Boreham Wood	27	10	8	9	29	25	4	38
13. Bromley	27	11	5	11	34	36	-2	38
14. Sutton United	26	10	5	11	30	34	-4	35
15. Solihull Moors	26	9	6	11	38	43	-5	33
16. Wrexham	27	8	8	11	24	35	-11	32
17. Torquay	26	8	6	12	30	37	-7	30
18. Braintree	25	7	6	12	29	43	-14	27
19. Southport	26	7	6	13	32	54	-22	27
20. Maidstone United	27	7	5	15	30	51	-21	26
21. Woking	26	6	6	14	37	50	-13	24
22. North Ferriby	27	7	3	17	14	38	-24	24
23. GUISELEY	**27**	**5**	**7**	**15**	**30**	**44**	**-14**	**22**
24. York	27	4	9	14	23	44	-21	21

Habergham (og) Boyes Power Williams Marriott for Robinson Palmer Power (pen) Hawkridge Wood Boyes Muldoon for Power Raggett Lowe Arnold Purver for Preston Green for Walton Howe for Rhead

1 2 3 4 5 6 7 8 9 10 11 12 13 14 15 16 17 18 19 20 21 22 23 24 25 26 27 28 29 30 31 32 33 34 35 36 37 38 39 40 41 42 43 44 45 46 47 48 49 50 51 52 53 54 55 56 57 58 59 60 61 62 63 64 65 66 67 68 69 70 71 72 73 74 75 76 77 78 79 80 81 82 83 84 85 86 87 88 89 90

KEY POINTS: Guiseley manager Adam Lockwood sent to the stands in the 90th minute

KEY POINTS: Sub debut for Sean Long (on loan from Reading)

IPSWICH TOWN 2
LINCOLN CITY 2

Emirates FA Cup Third Round
Portman Road | 07.01.17

IPSWICH TOWN		LINCOLN CITY	
Dean GERKEN	1	1	Paul FARMAN
Jonas KNUDSON	3	2	Bradley WOOD
Christophe BERRA	6	3	Sam HABERGHAM
Brett PITMAN	11	5	Luke WATERFALL
Adam WEBSTER	15	8	Alan POWER
Kevin BRU	17	9	Matt RHEAD
Grant WARD	18	11	Terry HAWKRIDGE
Freddie SEARS	20	25	Sean RAGGETT
Andre DOZZELL	23	28	Nathan ARNOLD
Tom LAWRENCE	27	30	Alex WOODYARD
Josh EMMANUEL	29	31	Theo ROBINSON
subs		*subs*	
Jonathan DOUGLAS	22	7	Jack MULDOON
Shane McLOUGHLIN	25	10	Adam MARRIOTT
Adam McDONNELL	26	12	Sean LONG
Ben MORRIS	32	14	Taylor MILES
George FOWLER	40	22	Jack FIXTER
Pat WEBBER	41	27	Jamie McCOMBE
Bartosz BIALKOWSKI	33	23	Jimmy WALKER

REFEREE: Lee Probert
ASSISTANTS: Neil Davies & Marc Wilson
FOURTH OFFICIAL: Nick Kinseley
ATTENDANCE: 16,027 (4,838 City supporters)

Robinson   Lawrence

Robinson
Robinson   Muldoon for Robinson   Lawrence   Long for Rhead
                                                  Habergham

STANDING ON STAIRWAY
STRICTLY PROHIBITED
GREENE KING
IPA
L10
HAWKRIDGE
11
.com
adidas

KEY POINTS: Full debuts for Sean Long & Joe Ward | Referee Scott Oldham replaced at half-time by Fourth Official Mary Ryan

GATESHEAD 1
LINCOLN CITY 3

Buildbase FA Trophy Second Round
International Stadium | 14.01.17

GATESHEAD			LINCOLN CITY
Dan HANFORD	13	1	Paul FARMAN
James BOLTON	2	3	Sam HABERGHAM
Manny SMITH	4	4	Elliott WHITEHOUSE
Liam HOGAN	5	6	Callum HOWE
Jamal FYFIELD	6	7	Jack MULDOON
Wes YORK	7	8	Alan POWER
Jordan BURROW	15	10	Adam MARRIOTT
Nyal BELL	18	11	Terry HAWKRIDGE
Gus MAFUTA	22	12	Sean LONG
Luke HANNANT	25	25	Sean RAGGETT
Paddy McLAUGHLIN	26	38	Joe WARD
subs		subs	
George SMITH	3	2	Bradley WOOD
Danny JOHNSON	9	9	Matt RHEAD
Sam JONES	10	24	Jack McMENEMY
Toby AJALA	14	27	Jamie McCOMBE
Shaun MACDONALD	23	30	Alex WOODYARD
Bartosz BIALKOWSKI	33	23	Jimmy WALKER

REFEREE: Scott Oldham
ASSISTANTS: Adam Burgess & Alan Hull
FOURTH OFFICIAL: Mark Ryan
ATTENDANCE: 578 (169 City supporters)

Burrow

Habergham

Fyfield
Jones for Bell

Wood for Power

Whitehouse

Hawkridge
Ajala for Hannant
Woodyard for Hawkridge

Rhead for Marriott

Bolton

LINCOLN CITY 1
IPSWICH TOWN 0

Emirates FA Cup Third Round Replay
Sincil Bank Stadium | 17.01.17

LINCOLN CITY			IPSWICH TOWN
Paul FARMAN	1	1	Dean GERKEN
Bradley WOOD	2	3	Jonas KNUDSON
Sam HABERGHAM	3	4	Luke CHAMBERS
Luke WATERFALL	5	6	Christophe BERRA
Alan POWER	8	8	Cole SKUSE
Matt RHEAD	9	9	Leon BEST
Terry HAWKRIDGE	11	14	Paul DIGBY
Sean RAGGETT	25	18	Grant WARD
Nathan ARNOLD	28	22	Jonathan DOUGLAS
Alex WOODYARD	30	27	Tom LAWRENCE
Theo ROBINSON	31	29	Josh EMMANUEL
subs		*subs*	
Jack MULDOON	7	17	Kevin BRU
Adam MARRIOTT	10	20	Freddie SEARS
Sean LONG	12	23	Andre DOZZELL
Taylor MILES	14	26	Adam McDONNELL
Jamie McCOMBE	27	32	Ben MORRIS
Jack WEATHERELL	29	41	Pat WEBBER
Jimmy WALKER	23	33	Bartosz BIALKOWSKI

REFEREE: Ben Toner
ASSISTANTS: Billy Smallwood & Alix Pashley
FOURTH OFFICIAL: Mark Haywood
ATTENDANCE: 9,069 (1,094 visiting supporters)

Rhead

Douglas

Sears for Best ⚽ Dozzell for Ward

Marriott for Robinson

Wood
Arnold
Muldoon for Arnold
McCombe for Hawkridge

1 2 3 4 5 6 7 8 9 10 11 12 13 14 15 16 17 18 19 20 21 22 23 24 25 26 27 28 29 30 31 32 33 34 35 36 37 38 39 40 41 42 43 44 45 46 47 48 49 50 51 52 53 54 55 56 57 58 59 60 61 62 63 64 65 66 67 68 69 70 71 72 73 74 75 76 77 78 79 80 81 82 83 84 85 86 87 88 89 90

KEY POINTS: Game shown live on BBC One | Kick-off time 8.05pm | Minute's applause prior to kick-off & 76th minute tribute in memory of Graham Taylor | LCFC reach FA Cup Fourth Round for first time since the 1975/76 season

LINCOLN CITY 2
DOVER ATHLETIC 0

Sincil Bank Stadium | 20.01.17

LINCOLN CITY		DOVER ATHLETIC	
Paul FARMAN	1	18	Steve ARNOLD
Sam HABERGHAM	3	2	Sam MAGRI
Elliott WHITEHOUSE	4	3	Aswad THOMAS
Luke WATERFALL	5	5	Connor ESSAM
Matt RHEAD	9	6	Richard ORLU
Adam MARRIOTT	10	9	Ricky MILLER
Terry HAWKRIDGE	11	15	Jamie GRIMES
Sean LONG	12	16	Tyrone STERLING
Sean RAGGETT	25	17	Moses EMMANUEL
Nathan ARNOLD	28	25	Ross LAFAYETTE
Alex WOODYARD	30	27	James HURST
subs		*subs*	
Bradley WOOD	2	4	Chris KINNEAR
Callum HOWE	6	10	Tyrone MARSH
Alan POWER	8	11	Mitchell PINNOCK
Theo ROBINSON	31	23	Jack PARKINSON
Joe WARD	38	26	Joe HEALY

REFEREE: Anthony Backhouse
ASSISTANTS: Matthew Smith & Grant Taylor
FOURTH OFFICIAL: Robert Massey-Ellis
ATTENDANCE: 6,491 (85 visiting supporters)

TEAM	P	W	D	L	F	A	GD	PTS
1. LINCOLN CITY	**27**	**18**	**4**	**5**	**57**	**26**	**31**	**58**
2. Forest Green	28	15	8	5	57	33	24	53
3. Tranmere	27	16	5	6	38	22	16	53
4. Dag & Red	28	16	4	8	47	31	16	52
5. DOVER	**29**	**15**	**4**	**10**	**58**	**45**	**13**	**49**
6. Barrow	26	12	10	4	41	25	16	46
7. Aldershot	28	13	6	9	36	28	8	45
8. Macclesfield	26	13	4	9	38	27	11	43
9. Gateshead	28	11	9	8	45	29	16	42
10. Chester	28	11	9	8	44	34	10	42
11. Boreham Wood	28	11	8	9	30	25	5	41
12. Eastleigh	27	10	10	7	41	34	7	40
13. Bromley	28	11	5	12	35	41	-6	38
14. Wrexham	29	10	8	11	27	36	-9	38
15. Sutton United	27	10	5	12	30	35	-5	35
16. Solihull Moors	27	9	6	12	38	45	-7	33
17. Torquay	28	8	6	14	31	40	-9	30
18. Braintree	28	8	6	14	31	48	-17	30
19. Southport	28	8	6	14	34	56	-22	30
20. Woking	28	7	6	15	40	53	-13	27
21. Maidstone United	28	7	5	16	31	53	-22	26
22. Guiseley	28	6	7	15	32	45	-13	25
23. North Ferriby	29	7	3	19	14	43	-29	24
24. York	28	4	10	14	25	46	-21	22

Sterling (og)

Robinson for Rhead

Healy for Hurst
Power for Marriott

Hawkridge
Wood for Hawkridge
Marsh for Emmanuel

Magri

KEY POINTS: Game shown live on BT Sport

PRE-MATCH PREPARATIONS
Behind the scenes prior to the FA Cup Replay against Ipswich Town

BARROW 3
LINCOLN CITY 0

Furness Building Society Stadium | 24.01.17

BARROW		LINCOLN CITY
Jon FLATT	40	1 Paul FARMAN
Shaun BEELEY	2	2 Bradley WOOD
Nick ANDERTON	3	5 Luke WATERFALL
Danny LIVESEY	5	8 Alan POWER
Moussa DIARRA	6	9 Matt RHEAD
Alex-Ray HARVEY	8	11 Terry HAWKRIDGE
Richie BENNETT	9	12 Sean LONG
Jordan WILLIAMS	11	25 Sean RAGGETT
Paul TURBULL	17	28 Nathan ARNOLD
Byron HARRISON	20	30 Alex WOODYARD
Akil WRIGHT	23	31 Theo ROBINSON
subs		subs
Ross HANNAH	10	4 Elliott WHITEHOUSE
Lindon MEIKLE	16	6 Callum HOWE
Liam HUGHES	18	7 Jack MULDOON
Dan ROWE	21	10 Adam MARRIOTT
Myles ANDERSON	25	38 Joe WARD

REFEREE: Tom Bramall
ASSISTANTS: Richard Woodward & Mark Cunliffe
FOURTH OFFICIAL: Will Finnie
ATTENDANCE: 1,152 (124 City supporters)

TEAM	P	W	D	L	F	A	GD	PTS
1. LINCOLN CITY	27	18	4	5	57	26	31	58
2. Forest Green	28	15	8	5	57	33	24	53
3. Tranmere	27	16	5	6	38	22	16	53
4. Dag & Red	28	16	4	8	47	31	16	52
5. Dover	29	15	4	10	58	45	13	49
6. BARROW	26	12	10	4	41	25	16	46
7. Aldershot	28	13	6	9	36	28	8	45
8. Macclesfield	26	13	4	9	38	27	11	43
9. Gateshead	28	11	9	8	45	29	16	42
10. Chester	28	11	9	8	44	34	10	42
11. Boreham Wood	28	11	8	9	30	25	5	41
12. Eastleigh	27	10	10	7	41	34	7	40
13. Bromley	28	11	5	12	35	41	-6	38
14. Wrexham	29	10	8	11	27	36	-9	38
15. Sutton United	27	10	5	12	30	35	-5	35
16. Solihull Moors	27	9	6	12	38	45	-7	33
17. Torquay	28	8	6	14	31	40	-9	30
18. Braintree	28	8	6	14	31	48	-17	30
19. Southport	28	8	6	14	34	56	-22	30
20. Woking	28	7	6	15	40	53	-13	27
21. Maidstone United	28	7	5	16	31	53	-22	26
22. Guiseley	28	6	7	15	32	45	-13	25
23. North Ferriby	29	7	3	19	14	43	-29	24
24. York	28	4	10	14	25	46	-21	22

Harrison

Hughes for Harrison
Bennett

Whitehouse for Power
Ward for Hawkridge
Bennett

Rhead
Marriott for Rhead
Turnbull
Raggett
Whitehouse

Hannah for Williams
Hannah (pen)

LINCOLN CITY 3
BRIGHTON & HOVE ALBION 1

Emirates FA Cup Fourth Round
Sincil Bank Stadium | 28.01.17

LINCOLN CITY			BRIGHTON & HOVE ALBION
Paul FARMAN	1	1	Niki MAENPAA
Bradley WOOD	2	4	Uwe HUENEMEIER
Sam HABERGHAM	3	8	Jiri SKALAK
Luke WATERFALL	5	14	Steve SIDWELL
Alan POWER	8	17	Glenn MURRAY
Matt RHEAD	9	18	Connor GOLDSON
Terry HAWKRIDGE	11	20	Solly MARCH
Sean RAGGETT	25	21	Oliver NORWOOD
Nathan ARNOLD	28	27	Fikayo TOMORI
Alex WOODYARD	30	29	Richie TOWELL
Theo ROBINSON	31	44	Sam ADEKUGBE
subs		subs	
Jack MULDOON	7	5	Lewis DUNK
Adam MARRIOTT	10	7	Beram KAYAL
Sean LONG	12	10	Tomer HEMED
Taylor MILES	14	15	Jamie MURPHY
Jamie McCOMBE	27	24	Rohan INCE
Archie MOYSES	35	43	Benjamin WHITE
Jimmy WALKER	23	16	Casper ANKERGREN

REFEREE: Andy Madley
ASSISTANTS: James Wilson & Philip Dermott
FOURTH OFFICIAL: Mark Brown
ATTENDANCE: 9,469 (1,391 visiting supporters)

KEY POINTS: Match broadcast live on BBC Radio Five Live & Talksport Radio and featured as lead game on BBC TV's Match Of The Day | BBC TV's Football Focus programme broadcast live from Sincil Bank

SOLIHULL MOORS 0
LINCOLN CITY 1
The Automated Technology Stadium | 31.01.17

SOLIHULL MOORS		LINCOLN CITY	
Nathan BAXTER	24	1	Paul FARMAN
Shepherd MUROMBEDZI	2	2	Bradley WOOD
Liam DALY	4	3	Sam HABERGHAM
Joel KETTLE	5	4	Elliott WHITEHOUSE
Calum FLANAGAN	6	5	Luke WATERFALL
Ashley SAMMONS	7	7	Jack MULDOON
Kristian GREEN	12	9	Matt RHEAD
Simeon MAYE	14	11	Terry HAWKRIDGE
Harry WHITE	19	25	Sean RAGGETT
George CARLINE	25	28	Nathan ARNOLD
Nortei NORTEY	31	30	Alex WOODYARD
subs			*subs*
Jack BYRNE	8	8	Alan POWER
Luke RODGERS	11	10	Adam MARRIOTT
Pearson MWANYONGO	18	12	Sean LONG
Omari STERLING-JAMES	22	36	Josh GINNELLY
Danny LEWIS	1	38	Joe WARD

REFEREE: Antony Coggins
ASSISTANTS: Matthew Smith & Sam Lewis
FOURTH OFFICIAL: Robert Claussen
ATTENDANCE: 1,650 (1,164 City supporters)

TEAM	P	W	D	L	F	A	GD	PTS
1. LINCOLN CITY	**29**	**19**	**4**	**6**	**58**	**29**	**29**	**61**
2. Forest Green	30	16	9	5	61	36	25	57
3. Tranmere	29	17	5	7	41	24	17	56
4. Dag & Red	29	17	4	8	49	31	18	55
5. Dover	30	16	4	10	61	46	15	52
6. Barrow	29	13	10	6	47	30	17	49
7. Aldershot	30	13	8	9	37	29	8	47
8. Macclesfield	28	14	4	10	41	29	12	46
9. Gateshead	30	11	10	9	47	33	14	43
10. Chester	30	11	10	9	46	38	8	43
11. Boreham Wood	30	11	9	10	31	27	4	42
12. Wrexham	31	11	9	11	30	38	-8	42
13. Eastleigh	29	10	11	8	42	36	6	41
14. Bromley	29	12	5	12	38	42	-4	41
15. SOLIHULL MOORS	**30**	**10**	**7**	**13**	**40**	**46**	**-6**	**37**
16. Sutton United	28	10	6	12	31	36	-5	36
17. Torquay	30	9	6	15	35	43	-8	33
18. Braintree	29	8	7	14	32	49	-17	31
19. Woking	30	8	6	16	41	56	-15	30
20. Southport	30	8	6	16	37	63	-26	30
21. Maidstone United	30	8	5	17	33	56	-23	29
22. Guiseley	29	7	7	15	34	46	-12	28
23. North Ferriby	31	8	3	20	18	47	-29	27
24. York	30	5	11	14	27	47	-20	26

White — Muldoon — Muldoon — Marriott for Muldoon — Rodgers for White / Power for Rhead / Kettle — Sterling-James for Nortey — Raggett — Mwanyongo for Sammons / Long for Arnold

KEY POINTS: Debuts for Dayle Southwell & Josh Ginnelly | First LCFC goals for Dayle Southwell and Joe Ward

WELLING UNITED 1
LINCOLN CITY 3

Buildbase FA Trophy Third Round
Park View Road | 04.02.17

WELLING UNITED			LINCOLN CITY
Chris LEWINGTON	1	1	Paul FARMAN
Matt FISH	2	4	Elliott WHITEHOUSE
Jordan BROWN	3	6	Callum HOWE
Sam HATTON	4	7	Jack MULDOON
Rickie HAYLES	5	8	Alan POWER
Sean FRANCIS	6	11	Terry HAWKRIDGE
Christian NANETTI	7	12	Sean LONG
Danny WALDREN	8	27	Jamie McCOMBE
Harry CRAWFORD	9	31	Dayle SOUTHWELL
Adam COOMBES	10	36	Josh GINNELLY
Pierre JOSEPH-DUBOIS	11	38	Joe WARD
subs		subs	
Jamie SLABBER	12	2	Bradley WOOD
Archie JOHNSON	14	10	Adam MARRIOTT
Ali FUSEINI	15	25	Sean RAGGETT
Dan WALKER	16	32	Luke ANDERSEN
Dean LEACOCK	17	23	Jimmy WALKER

REFEREE: Adrian Quelch
ASSISTANTS: Nick Dunn & Sam Ogles
FOURTH OFFICIAL: Graeme Ions
ATTENDANCE: 743

LINCOLN CITY 3
WOKING 2

Sincil Bank Stadium | 11.02.17

LINCOLN CITY		WOKING	
Paul FARMAN	1	1	Michael POKE
Bradley WOOD	2	2	Jake CAPRICE
Sam HABERGHAM	3	3	Terell THOMAS
Luke WATERFALL	5	4	Joey JONES
Matt RHEAD	9	6	Ismail YAKUBU
Terry HAWKRIDGE	11	8	Kieran MURTAGH
Sean RAGGETT	25	9	Gozie UGWU
Nathan ARNOLD	28	14	Fabio SARAIVA
Alex WOODYARD	30	22	Kane FERDINAND
Dayle SOUTHWELL	31	23	Macauley BONNE
Billy KNOTT	34	26	Chris ARTHUR
subs		*subs*	
Elliott WHITEHOUSE	4	12	Charlie CARTER
Alan POWER	8	15	Max KRETZSCHMAR
Adam MARRIOTT	10	16	Dennon LEWIS
Sean LONG	12	21	Luke KANDI
Josh GINNELLY	36	18	Brandon HALL

REFEREE: Sam Allison
ASSISTANTS: Jon Block & Callum Walchester
FOURTH OFFICIAL: Chris Francis
ATTENDANCE: 5,553 (64 visiting supporters)

TEAM	P	W	D	L	F	A	GD	PTS
1. LINCOLN CITY	**30**	**20**	**4**	**6**	**61**	**31**	**30**	**64**
2. Dag & Red	31	19	4	8	56	34	22	61
3. Forest Green	31	17	9	5	63	36	27	60
4. Tranmere	30	17	6	7	43	26	17	57
5. Dover	31	16	5	10	62	47	15	53
6. Aldershot	32	14	9	9	41	31	10	51
7. Barrow	30	13	11	6	49	32	17	50
8. Gateshead	32	13	10	9	52	34	18	49
9. Macclesfield	29	14	5	10	42	30	12	47
10. Wrexham	33	12	10	11	34	40	-6	46
11. Bromley	31	13	6	12	41	44	-3	45
12. Chester	32	11	10	11	49	43	6	43
13. Eastleigh	30	10	12	8	43	37	6	42
14. Boreham Wood	31	11	9	11	31	29	2	42
15. Solihull Moors	31	11	7	13	43	46	-3	40
16. Sutton United	29	10	6	13	31	39	-8	36
17. Torquay	32	9	7	16	36	45	-9	34
18. Braintree	30	9	7	14	33	49	-16	34
19. WOKING	**31**	**8**	**6**	**17**	**43**	**59**	**-16**	**30**
20. Maidstone United	32	8	6	18	34	59	-25	30
21. Southport	32	8	6	18	38	70	-32	30
22. Guiseley	31	7	8	16	36	50	-14	29
23. York	31	5	12	14	28	48	-20	27
24. North Ferriby	32	8	3	21	18	48	-30	27

Rhead
Ugwu
⚽⚽
Ferdinand
⚽
Yakubu
⚽

Ginnelly for Hawkridge
🔁
Ginnelly
⚽
Rhead
⚽
Carter for Murtagh
🔁
Whitehouse for Southwell
🔁
Saraiva (pen)
Power for Knott
⚽🔁
Kandi for Yakubu
🔁

rho

KEY POINTS: Debut for Billy Knott

KEY POINTS: Game shown live on BT Sport | Goal line technology used to confirm LCFC goal but referee did not have access to it | LCFC became the first non-League side to reach the Quarter Finals of The FA Cup in modern times

BURNLEY 0
LINCOLN CITY 1

Emirates FA Cup Fifth Round
Turf Moor | 18.02. 17

BURNLEY			LINCOLN CITY
Tom HEATON	1	1	Paul FARMAN
Jon FLANAGAN	4	2	Bradley WOOD
Michael KEANE	5	3	Sam HABERGHAM
Andre GRAY	7	5	Luke WATERFALL
Sam VOKES	9	7	Jack MULDOON
Ashley WESTWOOD	18	8	Alan POWER
Joey BARTON	19	9	Matt RHEAD
Johann BERG GUNDMUNDSSON	25	11	Terry HAWKRIDGE
James TARKOWSKI	26	25	Sean RAGGETT
Tendayi DARIKWA	27	28	Nathan ARNOLD
Scott ARFIELD	37	30	Alex WOODYARD
subs		subs	
Matt LOWTON	2	10	Adam MARRIOTT
Ben MEE	6	12	Sean LONG
Ashley BARNES	10	24	Jack McMENEMY
George BOYD	21	27	Jamie McCOMBE
Stephen WARD	23	31	Dayle SOUTHWELL
Daniel AGYEI	32	38	Joe WARD
Paul ROBINSON	17	21	Richard WALTON

REFEREE: Graham Scott
ASSISTANTS: Simon Bennett & Jake Collin
FOURTH OFFICIAL: Peter Bankes
ATTENDANCE: 19,185 (3,213 City supporters)

Power

Boyd for Gudmundsson

Southwell for Muldoon

Barton
Wood

Barnes for Vokes

Ward for Hawkridge

Raggett
Barnes
McCombe for Rhead

UP FOR THE CUP!

First tie out of the hat in the Emirates FA Cup Fifth Round draw and City are paired with Burnley

Terry Hawkridge and Paul Farman pictured with the FA Cup on the wing of a Red Arrow!

Getting up close with the famous trophy

It's either Sutton United or Arsenal v Lincoln City in the FA Cup Quarter Finals – only the Cowley brothers manage to keep their cool!

On the eve of the Arsenal game, Gunners' legend Thierry Henry gets the chance to rub shoulders with Sean Raggett and Nathan Arnold

Jack Muldoon and close pal Jake Quickenden in relaxed mood ahead of the Burnley tie

KEY POINTS: LCFC's first visit to the ground | Record home attendance for North Ferriby United

NORTH FERRIBY UNITED 0
LINCOLN CITY 1

Eon Visual Media Stadium | 21.02.17

NORTH FERRIBY UNITED			LINCOLN CITY
Rory WATSON	1	1	Paul FARMAN
Sam TOPLISS	2	3	Sam HABERGHAM
Mark GRAY	5	4	Elliott WHITEHOUSE
Sam COSGROVE	7	5	Luke WATERFALL
Curtis BATESON	8	12	Sean LONG
Taron HARE	12	25	Sean RAGGETT
Ben MIDDLETON	15	28	Nathan ARNOLD
Robbie TINKLER	16	30	Alex WOODYARD
Jake SKELTON	20	31	Dayle SOUTHWELL
Matt DIXON	21	34	Billy KNOTT
Reece THOMPSON	25	36	Josh GINNELLY
subs			*subs*
Matty TEMPLETON	9	2	Bradley WOOD
Ryan KENDALL	10	7	Jack MULDOON
Ross ARMSTRONG	18	8	Alan POWER
Jordan COOKE	19	9	Matt RHEAD
Connor OLIVER	4	38	Joe WARD

REFEREE: Steve Rushton
ASSISTANTS: Dale Baines & Ben Speedie
FOURTH OFFICIAL: Aaron Bannister
ATTENDANCE: 2,389 (2,000+ City supporters)

TEAM	P	W	D	L	F	A	GD	PTS
1. LINCOLN CITY	**31**	**21**	**4**	**6**	**62**	**31**	**31**	**67**
2. Dag & Red	33	20	4	9	59	37	22	64
3. Tranmere	32	19	6	7	47	27	20	63
4. Forest Green	32	17	9	6	64	39	25	60
5. Dover	32	17	5	10	64	48	16	56
6. Gateshead	34	15	10	9	58	36	22	55
7. Barrow	32	14	12	6	50	32	18	54
8. Aldershot	33	15	9	9	43	31	12	54
9. Macclesfield	32	16	5	11	45	31	14	53
10. Wrexham	34	12	10	12	34	42	-8	46
11. Bromley	33	13	6	14	42	47	-5	45
12. Chester	33	11	10	12	51	47	4	43
13. Boreham Wood	33	11	10	12	33	32	1	43
14. Solihull Moors	33	12	7	14	45	48	-3	43
15. Eastleigh	33	10	12	11	43	42	1	42
16. Braintree	32	10	7	15	35	51	-16	37
17. Sutton United	30	10	6	14	32	41	-9	36
18. Torquay	33	9	8	16	36	45	-9	35
19. Guiseley	33	9	8	16	40	52	-12	35
20. Woking	33	9	7	17	45	60	-15	34
21. Maidstone United	33	9	6	18	38	61	-23	33
22. Southport	33	8	7	18	38	70	-32	31
23. York	33	5	13	15	30	52	-22	28
24. NORTH FERRIBY	**34**	**8**	**3**	**23**	**19**	**51**	**-32**	**27**

Waterfall

Dixon

Power for Knott
Kendall for Cosgrove
Rhead for Southwell

Templeton for Gray

Muldoon for Whitehouse

Oliver for Bateson

Power

KEY POINTS: LCFC reach The FA Trophy Semi-Finals for the first time

BOREHAM WOOD 0
LINCOLN CITY 2

Buildbase FA Trophy Quarter Final
Broughinge Road | 25.02.17

BOREHAM WOOD			LINCOLN CITY
Grant SMITH	1	1	Paul FARMAN
Danny WOODARDS	3	2	Bradley WOOD
Mark RICKETTS	4	3	Sam HABERGHAM
Matt PAINE	5	4	Elliott WHITEHOUSE
David STEPHENS	6	6	Callum HOWE
Kenny DAVIS	8	7	Jack MULDOON
Bruno ANDRADE	11	11	Terry HAWKRIDGE
Morgan FERRIER	12	12	Sean LONG
Anthony JEFFREY	14	27	Jamie McCOMBE
Femi ILESANMI	15	34	Billy KNOTT
Angelo BALANTA	19	38	Joe WARD
	subs	*subs*	
Ben NUNN	2	8	Alan POWER
Ricky SHAKES	7	10	Adam MARRIOTT
Jai REASON	10	31	Dayle SOUTHWELL
Ben GOODLIFFE	17	36	Josh GINNELLY
Jason WILLIAMS	23	23	Jimmy WALKER

REFEREE: Constantine Hatzidakis
ASSISTANTS: Sam Lewis & Andrew Williams
FOURTH OFFICIAL: Josh Smith
ATTENDANCE: 901 (576 City supporters)

Whitehouse · Williams for Balanta · Ward · Power for Knott · Ginnelly for Hawkridge · Paine (og) · Andrade · Reason for Woodards · Ginnelly · Habergham · Southwell for Muldoon · Shakes for Andrade

LINCOLN CITY 1
YORK CITY 1

Sincil Bank Stadium | 28.02.17

LINCOLN CITY		YORK CITY	
Paul FARMAN	1	28	Kyle LETHEREN
Sam HABERGHAM	3	3	Alex WHITTLE
Luke WATERFALL	5	8	Simon HESLOP
Alan POWER	8	9	Amari MORGAN-SMITH
Matt RHEAD	9	17	Asa HALL
Sean LONG	12	29	Vadaine OLIVER
Sean RAGGETT	25	31	Jon PARKIN
Nathan ARNOLD	28	33	Sean NEWTON
Alex WOODYARD	30	34	Adriano MOKE
Billy KNOTT	34	36	Daniel PARSLOW
Josh GINNELLY	36	37	Hamza BENCHERIF
subs		subs	
Bradley WOOD	2	2	Shaun ROONEY
Elliott WHITEHOUSE	4	7	Daniel NTI
Callum HOWE	6	12	Aidan CONNOLLY
Adam MARRIOTT	10	21	Scott FENWICK
Joe WARD	38	13	Luke SIMPSON

REFEREE: Karl Evans
ASSISTANTS: Hristo Karaivanov & Oliver Bickle
FOURTH OFFICIAL: Paul Buck
ATTENDANCE: 6,892 (196 visiting supporters)

TEAM	P	W	D	L	F	A	GD	PTS
1. LINCOLN CITY	32	21	5	6	63	32	31	68
2. Dag & Red	34	20	4	10	59	39	20	64
3. Tranmere	32	19	6	7	47	27	20	63
4. Forest Green	32	17	9	6	64	39	25	60
5. Dover	33	17	5	11	64	49	15	56
6. Gateshead	34	15	10	9	58	36	22	55
7. Aldershot	34	15	10	9	44	32	12	55
8. Barrow	33	14	12	7	50	33	17	54
9. Macclesfield	32	16	5	11	45	31	14	53
10. Wrexham	34	12	10	12	34	42	-8	46
11. Bromley	34	13	6	15	42	52	-10	45
12. Chester	33	11	10	12	51	47	4	43
13. Eastleigh	34	10	13	11	44	43	1	43
14. Boreham Wood	34	11	10	13	33	33	0	43
15. Solihull Moors	33	12	7	14	45	48	-3	43
16. Braintree	33	11	7	15	40	51	-11	40
17. Sutton United	31	11	6	14	33	41	-8	39
18. Guiseley	34	10	8	16	41	52	-11	38
19. Woking	34	10	7	17	46	60	-14	37
20. Maidstone United	34	10	6	18	40	61	-21	36
21. Torquay	33	9	8	16	36	45	-9	35
22. Southport	33	8	7	18	38	70	-32	31
23. YORK	34	5	14	15	31	53	-22	29
24. North Ferriby	34	8	3	23	19	51	-32	27

Parkin
Wood for Long

Parkin
Oliver
Howe for Raggett
Ward for Knott
Fenwick for Oliver

Power
Fenwick

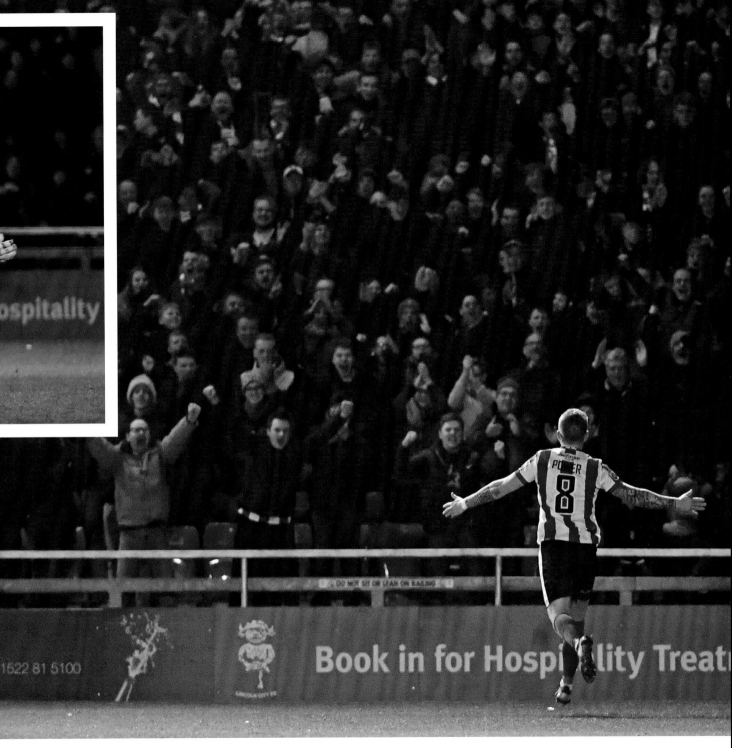

KEY POINTS: Debut for Billy Knott

ALDERSHOT TOWN 0
LINCOLN CITY 0

EBB Stadium | 04.03.17

ALDERSHOT TOWN			LINCOLN CITY
Jake COLE	1	1	Paul FARMAN
Nick ARNOLD	2	2	Bradley WOOD
Will EVANS	5	3	Sam HABERGHAM
Shamir FENELON	7	5	Luke WATERFALL
Scott RENDELL	9	8	Alan POWER
Bernard MENSAH	11	9	Matt RHEAD
Cheye ALEXANDER	12	11	Terry HAWKRIDGE
Jake GALLAGHER	16	13	Jonny MARGETTS
Idris KANU	19	25	Sean RAGGETT
Kundai BENYU	20	28	Nathan ARNOLD
Callum REYNOLDS	22	30	Alex WOODYARD
subs			subs
Anthony STRAKER	3	4	Elliott WHITEHOUSE
Matt McCLURE	10	6	Callum HOWE
Jonny GILES	21	7	Jack MULDOON
Callum BUCKLEY	23	34	Billy KNOTT
Mark SMITH	25	36	Josh GINNELLY

REFEREE: Craig Hicks
ASSISTANTS: Greg Read & Grant Taylor
FOURTH OFFICIAL: Craig Robson
ATTENDANCE: 3,595 (586 City supporters)

TEAM	P	W	D	L	F	A	GD	PTS
1. LINCOLN CITY	**33**	**21**	**6**	**6**	**63**	**32**	**31**	**69**
2. Forest Green	34	19	9	6	71	42	29	66
3. Tranmere	33	20	6	7	50	29	21	66
4. Dag & Red	35	20	4	11	59	40	19	64
5. Dover	35	18	6	11	67	49	18	60
6. ALDERSHOT	**36**	**16**	**11**	**9**	**48**	**32**	**16**	**59**
7. Gateshead	35	16	10	9	59	36	23	58
8. Barrow	34	14	13	7	50	33	17	55
9. Macclesfield	33	16	5	12	45	34	11	53
10. Wrexham	36	14	10	12	37	43	-6	52
11. Chester	35	12	10	13	54	50	4	46
12. Bromley	36	13	7	16	42	56	-14	46
13. Boreham Wood	35	11	11	13	33	33	0	44
14. Solihull Moors	35	12	8	15	45	49	-4	44
15. Eastleigh	36	10	13	13	45	49	-4	43
16. Sutton United	33	12	7	14	36	43	-7	43
17. Guiseley	36	11	8	17	44	55	-11	41
18. Braintree	35	11	8	16	41	53	-12	41
19. Maidstone United	36	11	7	18	44	63	-19	40
20. Woking	36	10	7	19	50	66	-16	37
21. Torquay	35	9	8	18	39	50	-11	35
22. North Ferriby	36	10	3	23	23	53	-30	33
23. York	35	6	14	15	34	54	-20	32
24. Southport	35	8	7	20	40	75	-35	31

Waterfall

Knott for Power
Arnold

Straker for Arnold

Ginnelly for Hawkridge

Muldoon for Margetts
Giles for Fenelon

McClure for Rendell

KEY POINTS: Debut for Lee Angol | First LCFC goals for Lee Angol | First time since 1966 that a player scored a hat-trick on LCFC debut

BRAINTREE TOWN 0
LINCOLN CITY 4

The IronmongeryDirect Stadium | 07.03.17

BRAINTREE TOWN			LINCOLN CITY
Sam BEASANT	22	1	Paul FARMAN
Jerome OKIMO	3	2	Bradley WOOD
Harry LEE	4	3	Sam HABERGHAM
Jack MIDSON	7	4	Elliott WHITEHOUSE
Reece HALL-JOHNSON	17	5	Luke WATERFALL
Sam CORNE	20	11	Terry HAWKRIDGE
Michael CHEEK	23	13	Jonny MARGETTS
Monty PATTERSON	24	25	Sean RAGGETT
Sean CLOHESSY	27	30	Alex WOODYARD
Manny PARRY	29	31	Lee ANGOL
Frankie MUSONDA	35	36	Josh GINNELLY
subs			*subs*
Lee BARNARD	9	6	Callum HOWE
Joe MAYBANKS	12	9	Matt RHEAD
Alex HENSHALL	15	10	Adam MARRIOTT
Claudio DIAS	25	28	Nathan ARNOLD
Kris TWARDEK	26	34	Billy KNOTT

REFEREE: Neil Hair
ASSISTANTS: Lee Brennan & Paul Saunders
FOURTH OFFICIAL: George Laflin
ATTENDANCE: 1,182 (384 City supporters)

TEAM	P	W	D	L	F	A	GD	PTS
1. LINCOLN CITY	34	22	6	6	67	32	35	72
2. Forest Green	34	19	9	6	71	42	29	66
3. Tranmere	34	20	6	8	51	31	20	66
4. Dag & Red	35	20	4	11	59	40	19	64
5. Dover	35	18	6	11	67	49	18	60
6. Aldershot	36	16	11	9	48	32	16	59
7. Gateshead	35	16	10	9	59	36	23	58
8. Barrow	35	15	13	7	52	34	18	58
9. Macclesfield	33	16	5	12	45	34	11	53
10. Wrexham	36	14	10	12	37	43	-6	52
11. Chester	35	12	10	13	54	50	4	46
12. Bromley	36	13	7	16	42	56	-14	46
13. Boreham Wood	35	11	11	13	33	33	0	44
14. Solihull Moors	35	12	8	15	45	49	-4	44
15. Eastleigh	36	10	13	13	45	49	-4	43
16. Sutton United	33	12	7	14	36	43	-7	43
17. Guiseley	36	11	8	17	44	55	-11	41
18. BRAINTREE	36	11	8	17	41	57	-16	41
19. Maidstone United	36	11	7	18	44	63	-19	40
20. Woking	36	10	7	19	50	66	-16	37
21. Torquay	35	9	8	18	39	50	-11	35
22. North Ferriby	36	10	3	23	23	53	-30	33
23. York	35	6	14	15	34	54	-20	32
24. Southport	35	8	7	20	40	75	-35	31

Angol

Angol

Waterfall

Howe for Waterfall

Arnold for Ginnelly
Rhead for Margetts

Maybanks for Corne

Angol (pen)

Arnold

Hendall for Patterson

KEY POINTS: Game shown live on BT Sport | Kick-off time 5.30pm | First time on teamsheet for Ross Etheridge and Riccardo Calder

ARSENAL 5
LINCOLN CITY 0

Emirates FA Cup Quarter Final
Emirates Stadium | 11.03. 17

ARSENAL			LINCOLN CITY
Petr CECH	33	1	Paul FARMAN
Kieran GIBBS	3	2	Bradley WOOD
Laurent KOSCIELNY	6	3	Sam HABERGHAM
ALEXIS Sanchez	7	5	Luke WATERFALL
Aaron RAMSEY	8	7	Jack MULDOON
Olivier GIROUD	12	8	Alan POWER
Theo WALCOTT	14	9	Matt RHEAD
Alex OXLADE-CHAMBERLAIN	15	11	Terry HAWKRIDGE
Shkodran MUSTAFI	20	25	Sean RAGGETT
Hector BELLERIN	24	28	Nathan ARNOLD
Granit XHAKA	29	30	Alex WOODYARD
subs		subs	
GABRIEL	5	10	Adam MARRIOTT
LUCAS Perez	9	13	Jonny MARGETTS
Mesut OZIL	11	24	Jack McMENEMY
Alex IWOBI	17	27	Jamie McCOMBE
Nacho MONREAL	18	37	Riccardo CALDER
Francis COQUELIN	34	38	Joe WARD
Emiliano MARTINEZ	26	39	Ross ETHERIDGE

REFEREE: Anthony Taylor
ASSISTANTS: Ian Hussin & Richard West
FOURTH OFFICIAL: Stuart Attwell
ATTENDANCE: 59,454 (8,942 City supporters)

KEY POINTS: Debut for Ross Etheridge

YORK CITY 2
LINCOLN CITY 1

Buildbase FA Trophy Semi Final First Leg
Bootham Crescent | 14.03.17

YORK CITY		LINCOLN CITY	
Kyle LETHEREN	28	39	Ross ETHERIDGE
Shaun ROONEY	2	2	Bradley WOOD
Alex WHITTLE	3	3	Sam HABERGHAM
Simon HESLOP	8	4	Elliott WHITEHOUSE
Amari MORGAN-SMITH	9	6	Callum HOWE
Scott FENWICK	21	10	Adam MARRIOTT
Vadaine OLIVER	29	27	Jamie McCOMBE
Jon PARKIN	31	31	Lee ANGOL
Sean NEWTON	33	34	Billy KNOTT
Danny HOLMES	35	36	Josh GINNELLY
Hamza BENCHERIF	37	38	Joe WARD
subs		subs	
Aidan CONNOLLY	12	5	Luke WATERFALL
Luke SIMPSON	13	7	Jack MULDOON
Tyler WALTON	16	8	Alan POWER
Sam FIELDING	30	9	Matt RHEAD
Adriano MOKE	34	11	Terry HAWKRIDGE

REFEREE: Anthony Backhouse
ASSISTANTS: Dean Chapman & Daniel Woodward
FOURTH OFFICIAL: Glen Hart
ATTENDANCE: 3,294 (1,358 City supporters)

LINCOLN CITY 1
YORK CITY 1
AET 2-3 ON AGGREGATE
Buildbase FA Trophy Semi Final Second Leg
Sincil Bank Stadium | 18.03.17

LINCOLN CITY			YORK CITY	
Paul FARMAN	1	28	Kyle LETHEREN	
Bradley WOOD	2	2	Shaun ROONEY	
Luke WATERFALL	5	8	Simon HESLOP	
Alan POWER	8	9	Amari MORGAN-SMITH	
Matt RHEAD	9	12	Aidan CONNOLLY	
Terry HAWKRIDGE	11	17	Asa HALL	
Sean RAGGETT	25	29	Vadaine OLIVER	
Nathan ARNOLD	28	31	Jon PARKIN	
Alex WOODYARD	30	33	Sean NEWTON	
Lee ANGOL	31	36	Daniel PARSLOW	
Riccardo CALDER	37	37	Hamza BENCHERIF	
subs		subs		
Elliott WHITEHOUSE	4	16	Tyler WALTON	
Adam MARRIOTT	10	21	Scott FENWICK	
Jonny MARGETTS	13	34	Adriano MOKE	
Billy KNOTT	34	35	Danny HOLMES	
Josh GINNELLY	36	13	Luke SIMPSON	

REFEREE: Ben Toner
ASSISTANTS: Alan Clayton & Neil Radford
FOURTH OFFICIAL: Danny Middleton
ATTENDANCE: 8,409 (694 visiting supporters)

KEY POINTS: After extra time | Debut for Riccardo Calder

MID-SEASON AWARDS

BOREHAM WOOD 2
LINCOLN CITY 0

Broughinge Road | 21.03.17

BOREHAM WOOD			LINCOLN CITY	
Grant SMITH	1	1	Paul FARMAN	
Ben NUNN	2	3	Sam HABERGHAM	
Danny WOODARDS	3	4	Elliott WHITEHOUSE	
Matt PAINE	5	5	Luke WATERFALL	
David STEPHENS	6	12	Sean LONG	
Ricky SHAKES	7	25	Sean RAGGETT	
Kenny DAVIS	8	28	Nathan ARNOLD	
Jai REASON	10	30	Alex WOODYARD	
Bruno ANDRADE	11	31	Lee ANGOL	
Femi ILESANMI	15	34	Billy KNOTT	
Joe DEVERA	33	36	Josh GINNELLY	
subs		subs		
Tom HITCHCOCK	9	2	Bradley WOOD	
Morgan FERRIER	12	8	Alan POWER	
Quba GORDON	22	9	Matt RHEAD	
Jason WILLIAMS	23	11	Terry HAWKRIDGE	
Frank KEITA	27	13	Jonny MARGETTS	

REFEREE: Carl Brook
ASSISTANTS: Michael Lowe & Nick Dunn
FOURTH OFFICIAL: Tom Bishop
ATTENDANCE: 1,002 (601 City supporters)

TEAM	P	W	D	L	F	A	GD	PTS
1. Forest Green	38	22	9	7	79	46	33	75
2. LINCOLN CITY	**35**	**22**	**6**	**7**	**67**	**34**	**33**	**72**
3. Tranmere	36	21	7	8	55	32	23	70
4. Dag & Red	38	21	4	13	63	46	17	67
5. Gateshead	39	18	12	9	65	39	26	66
6. Aldershot	39	18	11	10	53	34	19	65
7. Dover	37	19	6	12	68	54	14	63
8. Barrow	38	16	14	8	55	38	17	62
9. Macclesfield	35	17	6	12	49	37	12	57
10. Wrexham	39	14	11	14	38	49	-11	53
11. BOREHAM WOOD	**39**	**13**	**13**	**13**	**40**	**33**	**7**	**52**
12. Eastleigh	39	13	13	13	51	51	0	52
13. Bromley	38	14	7	17	45	57	-12	49
14. Solihull Moors	38	13	9	16	53	55	-2	48
15. Chester	37	12	10	15	56	54	2	46
16. Guiseley	39	12	10	17	46	56	-10	46
17. Sutton United	37	12	9	16	40	50	-10	45
18. Braintree	39	12	9	18	47	63	-16	45
19. Woking	39	11	8	20	54	69	-15	41
20. Maidstone United	37	11	8	18	45	64	-19	41
21. Torquay	38	10	9	19	43	54	-11	39
22. York	37	7	15	15	41	59	-18	36
23. North Ferriby	39	10	3	26	25	64	-39	33
24. Southport	38	8	7	23	44	84	-40	31

Reason

Rhead for Knott

Shakes

Hawkridge for Ginnelly
Margetts for Angol

Ferrier for Reason

Andrade

Ferrier
Hitchcock for Andrade

LINCOLN CITY 3
FOREST GREEN ROVERS 1

Sincil Bank Stadium | 25.03.17

LINCOLN CITY		FOREST GREEN ROVERS	
Paul FARMAN	1	23	Sam RUSSELL
Sam HABERGHAM	3	4	Drissa TRAORE
Luke WATERFALL	5	5	Mark ELLIS
Alan POWER	8	6	Dale BENNETT
Matt RHEAD	9	8	Sam WEDGBURY
Terry HAWKRIDGE	11	9	Christian DOIDGE
Sean LONG	12	10	Marcus KELLY
Sean RAGGETT	25	12	Darren CARTER
Nathan ARNOLD	28	14	Kaiyne WOOLERY
Alex WOODYARD	30	15	Liam NOBLE
Lee ANGOL	31	20	Charlie COOPER
subs		*subs*	
Elliott WHITEHOUSE	4	2	Curtis TILT
Callum HOWE	6	11	Omar BUGIEL
Adam MARRIOTT	10	19	Rob SINCLAIR
Harry ANDERSON	26	26	Fabien ROBERT
Billy KNOTT	34	31	Jake GOSLING

REFEREE: Antony Coggins
ASSISTANTS: Callum Walchester & Alex Guy
FOURTH OFFICIAL: Declan Bourne
ATTENDANCE: 6,798 (160 visiting supporters)

TEAM	P	W	D	L	F	A	GD	PTS
1. LINCOLN CITY	**36**	**23**	**6**	**7**	**70**	**35**	**35**	**75**
2. FOREST GREEN	**39**	**22**	**9**	**8**	**80**	**49**	**31**	**75**
3. Tranmere	37	22	7	8	56	32	24	73
4. Dag & Red	39	22	4	13	64	46	18	70
5. Aldershot	40	19	11	10	55	34	21	68
6. Gateshead	40	18	13	9	66	40	26	67
7. Dover	38	20	6	12	72	54	18	66
8. Barrow	39	17	14	8	59	40	19	65
9. Macclesfield	36	17	6	13	49	39	10	57
10. Wrexham	40	14	12	14	39	50	-11	54
11. Eastleigh	40	13	14	13	52	52	0	53
12. Boreham Wood	40	13	13	14	40	34	6	52
13. Chester	38	13	10	15	57	54	3	49
14. Bromley	39	14	7	18	45	58	-13	49
15. Solihull Moors	39	13	9	17	55	59	-4	48
16. Sutton United	38	13	9	16	45	51	-6	48
17. Guiseley	40	12	10	18	46	60	-14	46
18. Braintree	40	12	9	19	47	64	-17	45
19. Maidstone United	38	12	8	18	49	66	-17	44
20. Woking	40	11	8	21	56	73	-17	41
21. Torquay	39	10	10	19	44	55	-11	40
22. York	38	7	15	16	41	60	-19	36
23. Southport	39	9	7	23	45	84	-39	34
24. North Ferriby	40	10	3	27	26	69	-43	33

Doidge · Waterfall · Angol · Kelly (og) · Tilt for Traore · Anderson for Hawkridge · Habergham · Bugiel for Woolery · Robert for Wedgbury · Cooper · Whitehouse for Angol

SUTTON UNITED 1
LINCOLN CITY 1

Gander Green Lane | 28.03.17

SUTTON UNITED			LINCOLN CITY
Will PUDDY	26	1	Paul FARMAN
Kevin AMANKWAAH	2	3	Sam HABERGHAM
Louis JOHN	5	5	Luke WATERFALL
Jamie COLLINS	6	8	Alan POWER
Bedsente GOMIS	8	9	Matt RHEAD
Craig EASTMOND	15	11	Terry HAWKRIDGE
Nicky BAILEY	16	12	Sean LONG
Roarie DEACON	21	25	Sean RAGGETT
Maxime BIAMOU	24	28	Nathan ARNOLD
Adam COOMBES	30	30	Alex WOODYARD
Kieron CADOGAN	31	31	Lee ANGOL
subs			subs
Ben JEFFORD	3	2	Bradley WOOD
Adam MAY	12	4	Elliott WHITEHOUSE
Craig DUNDAS	14	10	Adam MARRIOTT
Dan SPENCE	17	26	Harry ANDERSON
Jeck JEBB	18	34	Billy KNOTT

REFEREE: Dean Treleaven
ASSISTANTS: Ben Cobb & Graeme Ions
FOURTH OFFICIAL: Paul Lister
ATTENDANCE: 2,246

TEAM	P	W	D	L	F	A	GD	PTS
1. LINCOLN CITY	37	23	7	7	71	36	35	76
2. Tranmere	38	23	7	8	57	32	25	76
3. Forest Green	39	22	9	8	80	49	31	75
4. Dag & Red	39	22	4	13	64	46	18	70
5. Aldershot	40	19	11	10	55	34	21	68
6. Barrow	40	18	14	8	61	41	20	68
7. Gateshead	40	18	13	9	66	40	26	67
8. Dover	39	20	6	13	72	55	17	66
9. Macclesfield	37	17	6	14	50	42	8	57
10. Wrexham	40	14	12	14	39	50	-11	54
11. Eastleigh	40	13	14	13	52	52	0	53
12. Boreham Wood	40	13	13	14	40	34	6	52
13. Chester	39	13	10	16	58	56	2	49
14. SUTTON UNITED	**39**	**13**	**10**	**16**	**46**	**52**	**-6**	**49**
15. Bromley	39	14	7	18	45	58	-13	49
16. Solihull Moors	40	13	9	18	55	60	-5	48
17. Guiseley	40	12	10	18	46	60	-14	46
18. Braintree	40	12	9	19	47	64	-17	45
19. Maidstone United	38	12	8	18	49	66	-17	44
20. Torquay	40	11	10	19	45	55	-10	43
21. Woking	40	11	8	21	56	73	-17	41
22. York	39	8	15	16	44	61	-17	39
23. Southport	39	9	7	23	45	84	-39	34
24. North Ferriby	40	10	3	27	26	69	-43	33

LINCOLN CITY 1
BROMLEY 0

Sincil Bank Stadium | 01.04.17

LINCOLN CITY			BROMLEY
Paul FARMAN	1	1	Ross FLITNEY
Sam HABERGHAM	3	4	Ben CHORLEY
Luke WATERFALL	5	5	Alan DUNNE
Alan POWER	8	6	Jack HOLLAND
Matt RHEAD	9	8	Lee MINSHULL
Sean LONG	12	9	George PORTER
Sean RAGGETT	25	13	Joe ANDERSON
Harry ANDERSON	26	14	Jordan HIGGS
Nathan ARNOLD	28	17	Blair TURGOTT
Alex WOODYARD	30	20	Tobi SHO-SILVA
Lee ANGOL	31	27	Shane McLOUGHLIN
subs		subs	
Bradley WOOD	2	3	Dan JOHNSON
Elliott WHITEHOUSE	4	10	Ryan HALL
Adam MARRIOTT	10	11	Louis DENNIS
Billy KNOTT	34	12	Connor DYMOND
Josh GINNELLY	36	19	Bradley GOLDBERG

REFEREE: Andrew Miller
ASSISTANTS: Richard Woodward & Iain Turner
FOURTH OFFICIAL: Neil Guest
ATTENDANCE: 6,843 (80 visiting supporters)

TEAM	P	W	D	L	F	A	GD	PTS
1. LINCOLN CITY	**38**	**24**	**7**	**7**	**72**	**36**	**36**	**79**
2. Tranmere	39	24	7	8	58	32	26	79
3. Forest Green	40	22	9	9	80	50	30	75
4. Dag & Red	40	23	4	13	68	46	22	73
5. Aldershot	41	20	11	10	57	34	23	71
6. Dover	40	21	6	13	74	55	19	69
7. Barrow	41	18	14	9	62	43	19	68
8. Gateshead	41	18	13	10	66	42	24	67
9. Macclesfield	38	18	6	14	54	44	10	60
10. Wrexham	41	14	12	15	39	51	-12	54
11. Eastleigh	41	13	14	14	52	56	-4	53
12. Boreham Wood	41	13	13	15	42	38	4	52
13. Chester	40	14	10	16	59	56	3	52
14. Sutton United	40	13	10	17	47	54	-7	49
15. Guiseley	41	13	10	18	47	60	-13	49
16. BROMLEY	**40**	**14**	**7**	**19**	**45**	**59**	**-14**	**49**
17. Solihull Moors	41	13	9	19	55	62	-7	48
18. Maidstone United	39	13	8	18	51	67	-16	47
19. Braintree	41	12	9	20	47	67	-20	45
20. Woking	41	12	8	21	58	74	-16	44
21. Torquay	41	11	10	20	45	56	-11	43
22. York	40	9	15	16	47	61	-14	42
23. North Ferriby	41	11	3	27	27	69	-42	36
24. Southport	40	9	7	24	45	85	-40	34

Johnson for Chorley
Waterfall
Turgott
Angol
Knott for Power
Knott
Ginnelly for Anderson
Dennis for McLouglin
Goldberg for Turgott
Whitehouse for Rhead
Raggett

KEY POINTS: Alan Power missed a 25th minute penalty | Billy Knott's first LCFC goal | 'Dam Buster' Johnny Johnson in attendance

LINCOLN CITY 2
DAGENHAM & REDBRIDGE 0

Sincil Bank Stadium | 03.04.17

LINCOLN CITY		DAGENHAM & REDBRIDGE	
Paul FARMAN	1	1	Elliot JUSTHAM
Bradley WOOD	2	3	Joe WIDDOWSON
Sam HABERGHAM	3	4	Scott DOE
Elliott WHITEHOUSE	4	5	Craig ROBSON
Luke WATERFALL	5	7	Luke HOWELL
Matt RHEAD	9	9	Elliott ROMAIN
Terry HAWKRIDGE	11	12	Oliver HAWKINS
Sean RAGGETT	25	17	Andre BOUCAUD
Nathan ARNOLD	28	25	Corey WHITELY
Alex WOODYARD	30	27	Shaun DONNELLAN
Lee ANGOL	31	32	Josh STAUNTON
subs		*subs*	
Adam MARRIOTT	10	8	Frankie RAYMOND
Sean LONG	12	10	Luke GUTTRIDGE
Harry ANDERSON	26	14	Paul BENSON
Billy KNOTT	34	15	Jordan MAGUIRE-DREW
Josh GINNELLY	36	30	Mark COUSINS

REFEREE: Anthony Backhouse
ASSISTANTS: Sam Lewis & Wayne Cartmel
FOURTH OFFICIAL: Garreth Rhodes
ATTENDANCE: 7,173 (145 visiting supporters)

TEAM	P	W	D	L	F	A	GD	PTS
1. LINCOLN CITY	**39**	**25**	**7**	**7**	**74**	**36**	**38**	**82**
2. Tranmere	39	24	7	8	58	32	26	79
3. Forest Green	40	22	9	9	80	50	30	75
4. DAG & RED	**41**	**23**	**4**	**14**	**68**	**48**	**20**	**73**
5. Aldershot	41	20	11	10	57	34	23	71
6. Dover	40	21	6	13	74	55	19	69
7. Barrow	41	18	14	9	62	43	19	68
8. Gateshead	41	18	13	10	66	42	24	67
9. Macclesfield	38	18	6	14	54	44	10	60
10. Wrexham	41	14	12	15	39	51	-12	54
11. Eastleigh	41	13	14	14	52	56	-4	53
12. Boreham Wood	41	13	13	15	42	38	4	52
13. Chester	40	14	10	16	59	56	3	52
14. Sutton United	40	13	10	17	47	54	-7	49
15. Guiseley	41	13	10	18	47	60	-13	49
16. Bromley	40	14	7	19	45	59	-14	49
17. Solihull Moors	41	13	9	19	55	62	-7	48
18. Maidstone United	39	13	8	18	51	67	-16	47
19. Braintree	41	12	9	20	47	67	-20	45
20. Woking	41	12	8	21	58	74	-16	44
21. Torquay	41	11	10	20	45	56	-11	43
22. York	40	9	15	16	47	61	-14	42
23. North Ferriby	41	11	3	27	27	69	-42	36
24. Southport	40	9	7	24	45	85	-40	34

Benson for Hawkins

Whitehouse

Widdowson

Maguire-Drew for Romain

Rhead

Knott for Rhead

Anderson for Hawkridge
Raymond for Howell

Knott

Marriott for Angol

1 2 3 4 5 6 7 8 9 10 11 12 13 14 15 16 17 18 19 20 21 22 23 24 25 26 27 28 29 30 31 32 33 34 35 36 37 38 39 40 41 42 43 44 45 46 47 48 49 50 51 52 53 54 55 56 57 58 59 60 61 62 63 64 65 66 67 68 69 70 71 72 73 74 75 76 77 78 79 80 81 82 83 84 85 86 87 88 89 90

Game shown live on BT Sport

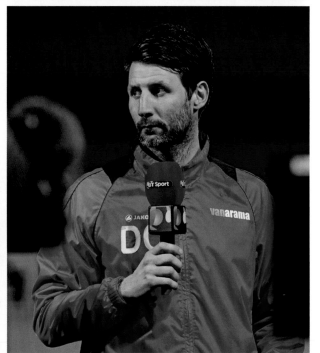

EASTLEIGH 0
LINCOLN CITY 1
Silverlake Stadium | 08.04.17

EASTLEIGH			LINCOLN CITY
Graham STACK	37	1	Paul FARMAN
Michael GREEN	3	2	Bradley WOOD
Adam DUGDALE	5	3	Sam HABERGHAM
Ben CLOSE	8	4	Elliott WHITEHOUSE
Sam MATTHEWS	12	5	Luke WATERFALL
Sam TOGWELL	14	9	Matt RHEAD
Paul REID	15	11	Terry HAWKRIDGE
Scott WILSON	18	25	Sean RAGGETT
Craig McALLISTER	19	28	Nathan ARNOLD
Gavin HOYTE	20	30	Alex WOODYARD
Hakeem ODOFFIN	29	31	Lee ANGOL
subs		subs	
Chinua COLE	2	8	Alan POWER
James CONSTABLE	9	10	Adam MARRIOTT
Matt TUBBS	10	12	Sean LONG
Ayo OBILEYE	24	26	Harry ANDERSON
Ben STREVENS	36	34	Billy KNOTT

REFEREE: Adam Bromley
ASSISTANTS: Stephen Brown & Aaron Moody
FOURTH OFFICIAL: Ryan Hillier-Smith
ATTENDANCE: 2,738 (659 City supporters)

TEAM	P	W	D	L	F	A	GD	PTS
1. LINCOLN CITY	40	26	7	7	75	36	39	85
2. Tranmere	41	26	7	8	70	34	36	85
3. Forest Green	41	23	9	9	81	50	31	78
4. Dag & Red	42	24	4	14	72	49	23	76
5. Aldershot	42	20	12	10	58	35	23	72
6. Dover	41	22	6	13	76	56	20	72
7. Barrow	42	18	15	9	64	45	19	69
8. Gateshead	42	18	13	11	67	44	23	67
9. Macclesfield	40	19	6	15	57	49	8	63
10. Boreham Wood	42	14	13	15	46	40	6	55
11. Bromley	42	16	7	19	51	62	-11	55
12. Wrexham	42	14	12	16	42	55	-13	54
13. EASTLEIGH	42	13	14	15	52	57	-5	53
14. Chester	41	14	10	17	59	58	1	52
15. Sutton United	42	13	11	18	51	59	-8	50
16. Maidstone United	40	14	8	18	53	68	-15	50
17. Guiseley	42	13	10	19	47	61	-14	49
18. Solihull Moors	42	13	9	20	55	71	-16	48
19. York	42	10	15	17	49	63	-14	45
20. Woking	42	12	9	21	60	76	-16	45
21. Braintree	42	12	9	21	48	69	-21	45
22. Torquay	42	11	11	20	46	57	-11	44
23. North Ferriby	42	11	3	28	29	73	-44	36
24. Southport	42	9	8	25	48	89	-41	35

Knott for Hawkridge
Tubbs for Matthews • Obiley for Wilson
Anderson for Whitehouse
Raggett
Wood
Power for Arnold
Constable for Close

LINCOLN CITY 1
CHESTER 0

Sincil Bank Stadium | 11.04.17

LINCOLN CITY		CHESTER	
Paul FARMAN	1	1	Alex LYNCH
Bradley WOOD	2	4	Luke GEORGE
Sam HABERGHAM	3	5	Blaine HUDSON
Elliott WHITEHOUSE	4	6	Ryan ASTLES
Luke WATERFALL	5	8	Tom SHAW
Matt RHEAD	9	9	James ALABI
Sean RAGGETT	25	10	Elliott DURRELL
Nathan ARNOLD	28	12	Sam HUGHES
Alex WOODYARD	30	14	Wade JOYCE
Lee ANGOL	31	15	Kane RICHARDS
Billy KNOTT	34	21	Ryan LLOYD
subs		subs	
Alan POWER	8	16	Johnny HUNT
Adam MARRIOTT	10	17	Theo VASSELL
Sean LONG	12	26	Lucas DAWSON
Harry ANDERSON	26	33	Liam DAVIES
Josh GINNELLY	36	13	Liam ROBERTS

REFEREE: Alan Young
ASSISTANTS: Paul Evans & Tom Hancock
FOURTH OFFICIAL: Andrew Dallison
ATTENDANCE: 7,401 (97 visiting supporters)

TEAM	P	W	D	L	F	A	GD	PTS
1. LINCOLN CITY	**41**	**27**	**7**	**7**	**76**	**36**	**40**	**88**
2. Tranmere	42	26	7	9	70	35	35	85
3. Forest Green	42	24	9	9	82	50	32	81
4. Dag & Red	42	24	4	14	72	49	23	76
5. Aldershot	42	20	12	10	58	35	23	72
6. Dover	41	22	6	13	76	56	20	72
7. Barrow	42	18	15	9	64	45	19	69
8. Gateshead	42	18	13	11	67	44	23	67
9. Macclesfield	41	20	6	15	60	49	11	66
10. Boreham Wood	42	14	13	15	46	40	6	55
11. Bromley	42	16	7	19	51	62	-11	55
12. Wrexham	42	14	12	16	42	55	-13	54
13. Eastleigh	42	13	14	15	52	57	-5	53
14. CHESTER	**42**	**14**	**10**	**18**	**59**	**59**	**0**	**52**
15. Sutton United	42	13	11	18	51	59	-8	50
16. Maidstone United	41	14	8	19	53	71	-18	50
17. Guiseley	42	13	10	19	47	61	-14	49
18. Solihull Moors	42	13	9	20	55	71	-16	48
19. York	42	10	15	17	49	63	-14	45
20. Woking	42	12	9	21	60	76	-16	45
21. Braintree	42	12	9	21	48	69	-21	45
22. Torquay	42	11	11	20	46	57	-11	44
23. North Ferriby	42	11	3	28	29	73	-44	36
24. Southport	42	9	8	25	48	89	-41	35

Anderson for Angol
Waterfall
Anderson
Durrell
Lloyd
Woodyard
Vassell for Hudson
Ginnelly for Knott
Power for Whitehouse
Power
Hunt for Joyce
Dawson for Lloyd
Richards
Farman
Dawson

1 2 3 4 5 6 7 8 9 10 11 12 13 14 15 16 17 18 19 20 21 22 23 24 25 26 27 28 29 30 31 32 33 34 35 36 37 38 39 40 41 42 43 44 45 46 47 48 49 50 51 52 53 54 55 56 57 58 59 60 61 62 63 64 65 66 67 68 69 70 71 72 73 74 75 76 77 78 79 80 81 82 83 84 85 86 87 88 89 90

LINCOLN CITY 2
TORQUAY UNITED 1

Sincil Bank Stadium | 14.04.17

LINCOLN CITY			TORQUAY UNITED
Paul FARMAN	1	1	Brendan MOORE
Sam HABERGHAM	3	3	Lathaniel ROWE-TURNER
Luke WATERFALL	5	4	Damon LATHROPE
Jack MULDOON	7	5	Giancarlo GALLIFUOCO
Matt RHEAD	9	8	Luke YOUNG
Sean LONG	12	12	Aman VERMA
Sean RAGGETT	25	15	Sean McGINTY
Nathan ARNOLD	28	17	Myles ANDERSON
Alex WOODYARD	30	18	Jamie REID
Billy KNOTT	34	19	Ruairi KEATING
Josh GINNELLY	36	31	Jordan LEE
subs		*subs*	
Bradley WOOD	2	6	Ben GERRING
Elliott WHITEHOUSE	4	7	Sam CHANEY
Adam MARRIOTT	10	9	Shaun HARRAD
Jonny MARGETTS	13	14	Brett WILLIAMS
Harry ANDERSON	26	33	Kevin NICHOLSON

REFEREE: Joe Johnson
ASSISTANTS: Darren Wilding & Mark Cunliffe
FOURTH OFFICIAL: Adam Burgess
ATTENDANCE: 9,011 (188 visiting supporters)

TEAM	P	W	D	L	F	A	GD	PTS
1. LINCOLN CITY	**42**	**28**	**7**	**7**	**78**	**37**	**41**	**91**
2. Tranmere	43	26	8	9	72	37	35	86
3. Forest Green	43	25	9	9	84	50	34	84
4. Dag & Red	43	25	4	14	75	50	25	79
5. Dover	42	23	6	13	79	56	23	75
6. Aldershot	43	20	13	10	60	37	23	73
7. Barrow	43	18	15	10	65	49	16	69
8. Gateshead	43	18	13	12	67	47	20	67
9. Macclesfield	42	20	6	16	60	50	10	66
10. Bromley	43	17	7	19	55	63	-8	58
11. Boreham Wood	43	14	13	16	47	43	4	55
12. Wrexham	43	14	12	17	43	58	-15	54
13. Sutton United	43	14	11	18	54	59	-5	53
14. Eastleigh	43	13	14	16	53	59	-6	53
15. Maidstone United	42	15	8	19	56	72	-16	53
16. Chester	43	14	10	19	59	61	-2	52
17. Guiseley	43	13	10	20	47	63	-16	49
18. York	43	11	15	17	51	64	-13	48
19. Woking	43	13	9	21	61	76	-15	48
20. Solihull Moors	43	13	9	21	56	73	-17	48
21. Braintree	43	13	9	21	50	69	-19	48
22. TORQUAY	**43**	**11**	**11**	**21**	**47**	**59**	**-12**	**44**
23. North Ferriby	43	12	3	28	31	74	-43	39
24. Southport	43	9	8	26	48	92	-44	35

KEY POINTS: Torquay's Shaun Harrad was cautioned whilst still on the bench as a substitute

KEY POINTS: Game shown live on BT Sport | Highest ever league attendance and away following for a game at the International Stadium

GATESHEAD 1
LINCOLN CITY 2

International Stadium | 17.04.17

GATESHEAD			LINCOLN CITY
Dan HANFORD	13	1	Paul FARMAN
James BOLTON	2	3	Sam HABERGHAM
George SMITH	3	4	Elliott WHITEHOUSE
Manny SMITH	4	5	Luke WATERFALL
Liam HOGAN	5	9	Matt RHEAD
Jamal FYFIELD	6	12	Sean LONG
Wes YORK	7	25	Sean RAGGETT
Jordan BURROW	15	26	Harry ANDERSON
Luke HANNANT	25	28	Nathan ARNOLD
Paddy McLAUGHLIN	26	30	Alex WOODYARD
JJ O'DONNELL	27	31	Lee ANGOL
subs		subs	
Mitch BRUNDLE	8	2	Bradley WOOD
Nyal BELL	18	7	Jack MULDOON
Jake WRIGHT	19	10	Adam MARRIOTT
Gus MAFUTA	22	34	Billy KNOTT
Shaun MACDONALD	23	36	Josh GINNELLY

REFEREE: Peter Wright
ASSISTANTS: Alan Hull & Hristo Karaivanov
FOURTH OFFICIAL: Dean Hulme
ATTENDANCE: 3,770 (2,486 City supporters)

TEAM	P	W	D	L	F	A	GD	PTS
1. LINCOLN CITY	43	29	7	7	80	38	42	94
2. Tranmere	44	27	8	9	74	38	36	89
3. Forest Green	44	25	9	10	84	52	32	84
4. Dag & Red	44	25	5	14	77	52	25	80
5. Aldershot	44	21	13	10	61	37	24	76
6. Dover	43	23	6	14	79	57	22	75
7. Barrow	44	19	15	10	68	50	18	72
8. GATESHEAD	44	18	13	13	68	49	19	67
9. Macclesfield	43	20	6	17	61	53	8	66
10. Bromley	44	17	7	20	56	65	-9	58
11. Wrexham	44	15	12	17	46	59	-13	57
12. Eastleigh	44	14	14	16	55	60	-5	56
13. Maidstone United	43	16	8	19	57	72	-15	56
14. Boreham Wood	44	14	13	17	47	44	3	55
15. Sutton United	44	14	12	18	56	61	-5	54
16. Chester	44	14	10	20	61	64	-3	52
17. Woking	44	14	9	21	64	78	-14	51
18. Solihull Moors	44	14	9	21	59	74	-15	51
19. Guiseley	44	13	10	21	48	65	-17	49
20. York	44	11	15	18	52	67	-15	48
21. Braintree	44	13	9	22	51	72	-21	48
22. Torquay	44	12	11	21	50	60	-10	41
23. North Ferriby	44	12	3	29	32	77	-45	39
24. Southport	44	10	8	26	50	92	-42	38

Raggett   McLaughlin (pen)   Marriott for Angol   Ginnelly for Anderson   Knott for Whitehouse   Hogan   O'Donnell   Brundle for O'Donnell   Rhead (pen)   York   Arnold   Arnold

LINCOLN CITY 2
MACCLESFIELD TOWN 1

Sincil Bank Stadium | 22.04.17

LINCOLN CITY		MACCLESFIELD TOWN	
Paul FARMAN	1	22	Scott FLINDERS
Bradley WOOD	2	2	Andy HALLS
Sam HABERGHAM	3	3	David FITZPATRICK
Elliott WHITEHOUSE	4	4	Neill BYRNE
Luke WATERFALL	5	5	George PILKINGTON
Matt RHEAD	9	7	Rhys BROWNE
Terry HAWKRIDGE	11	9	Chris HOLROYD
Sean RAGGETT	25	14	Kingsley JAMES
Nathan ARNOLD	28	15	Ollie NORBURN
Alex WOODYARD	30	16	Mitch HANCOX
Lee ANGOL	31	30	Luke SUMMERFIELD
subs		*subs*	
Adam MARRIOTT	10	6	John McCOMBE
Sean LONG	12	8	Danny WHITEHEAD
Harry ANDERSON	26	23	Danny WHITAKER
Billy KNOTT	34	29	Anthony DUDLEY
Josh GINNELLY	36	13	Craig ROSS

REFEREE: Tom Nield
ASSISTANTS: Matthew Smith & Martin Parker
FOURTH OFFICIAL: Simon Mather
ATTENDANCE: 10,031 (97 visiting supporters)

TEAM	P	W	D	L	F	A	GD	PTS
1. LINCOLN CITY	44	30	7	7	82	39	43	97
2. Tranmere	45	28	8	9	78	39	39	92
3. Forest Green	45	25	10	10	86	54	32	85
4. Dag & Red	45	26	5	14	78	52	26	83
5. Aldershot	45	22	13	10	64	37	27	79
6. Dover	44	23	6	15	80	59	21	75
7. Barrow	45	20	15	10	70	50	20	75
8. Gateshead	45	19	13	13	72	49	23	70
9. MACCLESFIELD	44	20	6	18	62	55	7	66
10. Bromley	45	17	8	20	57	66	-9	59
11. Sutton United	45	15	12	18	61	63	-2	57
12. Wrexham	45	15	12	18	46	60	-14	57
13. Maidstone United	44	16	9	19	59	74	-15	57
14. Eastleigh	45	14	14	17	55	62	-7	56
15. Boreham Wood	45	14	13	18	47	48	-1	55
16. Solihull Moors	45	15	9	21	61	74	-13	54
17. Chester	45	14	10	21	63	69	-6	52
18. Woking	45	14	10	21	65	79	-14	52
19. Torquay	45	13	11	21	52	61	-9	50
20. Guiseley	45	13	11	21	49	66	-17	50
21. York	45	11	16	18	53	68	-15	49
22. Braintree	45	13	9	23	51	74	-23	48
23. North Ferriby	45	12	3	30	32	80	-48	39
24. Southport	45	10	8	27	51	96	-45	38

MACCLESFIELD
TICKETS
SOLD OUT

KEY POINTS: Game shown live on BT Sport | Kick-off time 12.15pm | LCFC crowned Vanarama National League champions. Trophy presented by Brian Barwick, chairman of The National League | Record attendance at all-seated Sincil Bank

KEY POINTS: First visit to the Gallagher Stadium | Third different ground that LCFC have played against Maidstone United away from home

MAIDSTONE UNITED 0
LINCOLN CITY 0

Gallagher Stadium | 25.04.17

MAIDSTONE UNITED		LINCOLN CITY
Lee WORGAN	1	39 Ross ETHERIDGE
Tom MILLS	3	6 Callum HOWE
Kevin LOKKO	5	7 Jack MULDOON
Stuart LEWIS	8	8 Alan POWER
Alex FISHER	11	10 Adam MARRIOTT
Reece PRESTEDGE	14	11 Terry HAWKRIDGE
Harry PHIPPS	21	12 Sean LONG
Seth NANA-TWUMASI	22	25 Sean RAGGETT
Yemi ODUBADE	23	34 Billy KNOTT
Magnus OKUONGHAE	24	36 Josh GINNELLY
Joe PIGOTT	32	37 Riccardo CALDER
subs		*subs*
Jamie COYLE	4	2 Bradley WOOD
Jack PAXMAN	10	4 Elliott WHITEHOUSE
Anthony ACHEAMPONG	15	16 Alex SIMMONS
Bobby-Joe TAYLOR	16	27 Jamie McCOMBE
Jack RICHARDS	18	30 Alex WOODYARD

REFEREE: Constantine Hatzidakis
ASSISTANTS: Callum Walchester & Andrew Williams
FOURTH OFFICIAL: Conor Farrell
ATTENDANCE: 3,014 (598 City supporters)

TEAM	P	W	D	L	F	A	GD	PTS
1. LINCOLN CITY	**45**	**30**	**8**	**7**	**82**	**39**	**43**	**98**
2. Tranmere	45	28	8	9	78	39	39	92
3. Forest Green	45	25	10	10	86	54	32	85
4. Dag & Red	45	26	5	14	78	52	26	83
5. Aldershot	45	22	13	10	64	37	27	79
6. Dover	45	23	7	15	82	61	21	76
7. Barrow	45	20	15	10	70	50	20	75
8. Gateshead	45	19	13	13	72	49	23	70
9. Macclesfield	45	20	7	18	64	57	7	67
10. Bromley	45	17	8	20	57	66	-9	59
11. MAIDSTONE	**45**	**16**	**10**	**19**	**59**	**74**	**-15**	**58**
12. Sutton United	45	15	12	18	61	63	-2	57
13. Wrexham	45	15	12	18	46	60	-14	57
14. Eastleigh	45	14	14	17	55	62	-7	56
15. Boreham Wood	45	14	13	18	47	48	-1	55
16. Solihull Moors	45	15	9	21	61	74	-13	54
17. Chester	45	14	10	21	63	69	-6	52
18. Woking	45	14	10	21	65	79	-14	52
19. Torquay	45	13	11	21	52	61	-9	50
20. Guiseley	45	13	11	21	49	66	-17	50
21. York	45	11	16	18	53	68	-15	49
22. Braintree	45	13	9	23	51	74	-23	48
23. North Ferriby	45	12	3	30	32	80	-48	39
24. Southport	45	10	8	27	51	96	-45	38

Taylor for Phipps

Paxman for Lewis

Whitehouse for Marriott

Richards for Odubade

Richards
Simmons for Ginnelly

SOUTHPORT 1
LINCOLN CITY 1

Merseyrail Community Stadium | 29.04.17

SOUTHPORT		LINCOLN CITY	
Chris CHEETHAM	15	39	Ross ETHERIDGE
Neil ASHTON	3	5	Luke WATERFALL
Euan MURRAY	6	6	Callum HOWE
Jamie ALLEN	7	7	Jack MULDOON
Liam HYNES	10	8	Alan POWER
Ben McKENNA	14	9	Matt RHEAD
Declan WEEKS	19	11	Terry HAWKRIDGE
Rory McKEOWN	23	12	Sean LONG
Ryan HIGGINS	26	31	Lee ANGOL
Robbie CUNDY	24	34	Billy KNOTT
Spencer MYERS	29	36	Josh GINNELLY
subs		subs	
Jean COLY	11	4	Elliott WHITEHOUSE
Kevin MONTEIRO	16	16	Alex SIMMONS
Louis ALMOND	25	27	Jamie McCOMBE
Richard BRODIE	27	28	Nathan ARNOLD
Tom GRIMSHAW	30	30	Alex WOODYARD

REFEREE: Sam Allison
ASSISTANTS: Abbas Khan & Lee Freeman
FOURTH OFFICIAL: Lewis Raper
ATTENDANCE: 3,462 (2,458 City supporters)

TEAM	P	W	D	L	F	A	GD	PTS
1. LINCOLN CITY	46	30	9	7	83	40	43	99
2. Tranmere	46	29	8	9	79	39	40	95
3. Forest Green	46	25	11	10	88	56	32	86
4. Dag & Red	46	26	6	14	79	53	26	84
5. Aldershot	46	23	13	10	66	37	29	82
6. Dover	46	24	7	15	85	63	22	79
7. Barrow	46	20	15	11	72	53	19	75
8. Gateshead	46	19	13	14	72	51	21	70
9. Macclesfield	46	20	8	18	64	57	7	68
10. Bromley	46	18	8	20	59	66	-7	62
11. Boreham Wood	46	15	13	18	49	48	1	58
12. Sutton United	46	15	13	18	61	63	-2	58
13. Wrexham	46	15	13	18	47	61	-14	58
14. Maidstone United	46	16	10	20	59	75	-16	58
15. Eastleigh	46	14	15	17	56	63	-7	57
16. Solihull Moors	46	15	10	21	62	75	-13	55
17. Torquay	46	14	11	21	54	61	-7	53
18. Woking	46	14	11	21	66	80	-14	53
19. Chester	46	14	10	22	63	71	-8	52
20. Guiseley	46	13	12	21	50	67	-17	51
21. York	46	11	17	18	55	70	-15	50
22. Braintree	46	13	9	24	51	76	-25	48
23. SOUTHPORT	**46**	**10**	**9**	**27**	**52**	**97**	**-45**	**39**
24. North Ferriby	46	12	3	31	32	82	-50	39

171

OPEN TOP BUS TOUR

Tuesday 2 May 2017

CHAMPIONSHIP SEASON AWARDS DINNER

Lincolnshire Showground | Friday 19 May 2017

Harry Wilmot Memorial Trophy -
Young Player of the Season
SEAN RAGGETT

University of Lincoln Community
Player of the Season
PAUL FARMAN

Global Vision Goal of the Season
NATHAN ARNOLD v IPSWICH TOWN

Ray Hill Memorial Shield -
Voluntary Worker of the Season
ANDY HELGESEN

Twitter Player of the Season
ALEX WOODYARD

Lincolnshire Echo Player of the Season,
sponsored by Running Imp
ALEX WOODYARD

Bill Stacey Memorial Trophy –
Away Player of the Season
ALEX WOODYARD

Small Beer Champagne Moment of the Season
ALL OF THE 2016/17 SEASON!

Lifetime Achievement Award
GEORGE & DOREEN ASHTON

Player's Player of the Season, sponsored by
Travis Perkins
LUKE WATERFALL

Vic Withers Memorial Trophy -
Player of the Season
ALEX WOODYARD

VANARAMA NATIONAL LEAGUE 2016/17

Date	V	Opposition	Res	Crowd	Away	Pts	Pos	Referee	Scorers
Sat Aug 6	A	Woking	3-1	1,592	407	3	3	J Johnson	Marriott 27; Rhead 60, 72 pen
Tue Aug 9	H	North Ferriby United	6-1	3,622	113	6	1	R Whitton	Rhead 3, 24 pen; Arnold 5, Waterfall 16, Margetts 51, Wood 67
Sat Aug 13	H	Sutton United	1-3	3,195	81	6	4	S Barrow	Habergham 51
Tue Aug 16	A	Dagenham and Redbridge	0-1	1,399	247	6	14	D Treleaven	-
Sat Aug 20	A	Southport	4-0	2,440	69	9	8	A Coggins	Margetts 16, 30, 45+1, 80 pen
Sat Aug 27	A	Macclesfield Town	2-1	1,615	380	12	4	A Miller	Anderson 56, Marriott 75
Mon Aug 29	H	Gateshead	3-0	3,687	110	15	3	T Bramall	Raggett 6, Arnold 50, Marriott 84
Sat Sep 3	A	Torquay United	2-1	2,061	173	18	3	C Hicks	Rhead 3 pen, 90+3
Sat Sep 10	A	Tranmere Rovers	1-0	5,274	540	21	1	M Coy	Bonne 68
Tue Sep 13	H	Solihull Moors	0-0	4,049	22	22	1	T Nield	-
Sat Sep 17	A	Barrow	1-2	3,578	102	22	3	A Serrano	Arnold 33
Sat Sep 24	A	Dover Athletic	0-2	1,209	150	22	5	D Rock	-
Sat Oct 1	H	Braintree Town	3-0	3,554	66	25	4	S Rushton	Arnold 3, Waterfall 52, Muldoon 90
Tue Oct 4	A	Wrexham	2-1	3,487	137	28	2	S Allison	Waterfall 31, Anderson 45
Sat Oct 8	A	Bromley	1-1	1,511	304	29	3	A Serrano	Anderson 46
Sat Oct 22	H	Eastleigh	0-0	3,180	74	30	3	T Nield	-
Tue Oct 25	H	Boreham Wood	2-0	3,014	30	33	3	T Bramall	Arnold 45+6, Rhead 72
Sat Oct 29	A	Chester	5-2	2,486	413	36	2	A Backhouse	Robinson 41, Raggett 45+3, Rhead 47, Muldoon 81, Anderson 83
Sat Nov 12	H	Aldershot Town	3-3	3,461	159	37	2	M Coy	Arnold 21, 30; Rhead 90+6
Sat Nov 19	A	Forest Green Rovers	3-2	2,164	345	40	2	C Hatzidakis	Woodyard 68, Waterfall 89, Raggett 90+1
Tue Nov 22	A	York City	4-1	2,889	1,068	43	2	T Bramall	Whitehouse 24, Arnold 29, Waterfall 61, Wood 74
Sat Nov 26	H	Maidstone United	2-0	3,917	208	46	2	W Barratt	Robinson 52, Rhead 54
Tue Nov 29	H	Wrexham	1-0	3,344	75	49	1	D Rock	Whitehouse 14
Sat Dec 17	H	Tranmere Rovers	2-1	6,335	807	52	1	C Hicks	Arnold 33, Marriott 81
Mon Dec 26	A	Guiseley	1-2	2,446	974	52	2	A Miller	Waterfall 28
Sun Jan 1	H	Guiseley	3-1	5,148	101	55	1	C O'Donnell	Power 57 pen, Raggett 88, Arnold 90
Fri Jan 20	H	Dover Athletic	2-0	6,491	85	58	1	A Backhouse	Sterling 9 OG, Hawkridge 83
Tue Jan 24	A	Barrow	0-3	1,152	124	58	1	T Bramall	-
Tue Jan 31	A	Solihull Moors	1-0	1,650	1,164	61	1	A Coggins	Muldoon 51
Sat Feb 11	H	Woking	3-2	5,553	64	64	1	S Allison	Rhead 9, 60; Thomas 51 OG
Tue Feb 21	A	North Ferriby United	1-0	2,389	2,000+	67	1	S Rushton	Waterfall 21
Tue Feb 28	H	York City	1-1	6,892	196	68	1	K Evans	Power 76
Sat Mar 4	A	Aldershot Town	0-0	3,595	586	69	1	C Hicks	-
Tue Mar 7	A	Braintree Town	4-0	1,182	384	72	1	N Hair	Angol 15, 22, 82 pen; Arnold 85
Tue Mar 21	A	Boreham Wood	0-2	1,002	601	72	2	C Brook	-
Sat Mar 25	H	Forest Green Rovers	3-1	6,798	160	75	1	A Coggins	Angol 55, Kelly 61 OG, Habergham 75
Tue Mar 28	A	Sutton United	1-1	2,246		76	1	D Treleaven	Whitehouse 81
Sat Apr 1	H	Bromley	1-0	6,843	80	79	1	A Miller	Knott 66
Mon Apr 3	H	Dagenham and Redbridge	2-0	7,173	145	82	1	A Backhouse	Whitehouse 47, Rhead 68
Sat Apr 8	A	Eastleigh	1-0	2,738	659	85	1	A Bromley	Raggett 77
Tue Apr 11	H	Chester	1-0	7,401	97	88	1	A Young	Anderson 35
Fri Apr 14	H	Torquay United	2-1	9,011	188	91	1	J Johnson	Anderson 86, Habergham 88
Mon Apr 17	A	Gateshead	2-1	3,770	2,486	94	1	P Wright	Rhead 90 pen, Arnold 90+3
Sat Apr 22	H	Macclesfield Town	2-1	10,031	97	97	C	T Nield	Hawkridge 28, 76
Tue Apr 25	A	Maidstone United	0-0	3,014	598	98	C	C Hatzidakis	-
Sat Apr 29	A	Southport	1-1	3,462	2,458	99	C	S Allison	Angol 32

EMIRATES FA CUP 2016/17

Date	V	Opposition	Rd	Res	Crowd	Away	Referee	Scorers
Sat Oct 15	H	Guiseley	4Q	0-0	2,629	80	K Evans	-
Tue Oct 18	A	Guiseley	4QR	2-1	765	177	A Miller	Robinson 40, 51
Sat Nov 5	H	Altrincham	1	2-1	3,529	161	S Rushton	Raggett 21, Power 60
Mon Dec 5	H	Oldham Athletic	2	3-2	7,012	415	G Ward	Robinson 22, 47; Hawkridge 24
Sat Jan 7	A	Ipswich Town	3	2-2	16,027	4,838	L Probert	Robinson 7, 65
Tue Jan 17	H	Ipswich Town	3R	1-0	9,069	1,094	B Toner	Arnold 90+1
Sat Jan 28	H	Brighton & HA	4	3-1	9,469	1,391	A Madley	Power 57 pen, Tomori 62 OG, Robinson 85
Sat Feb 18	A	Burnley	5	1-0	19,185	3,213	G Scott	Raggett 89
Sat Mar 11	A	Arsenal	QF	0-5	59,454	8,942	A Taylor	-

BUILDBASE FA TROPHY 2016/17

Date	V	Opposition	Rd	Res	Crowd	Away	Referee	Scorers
Tue Dec 20	A	Nantwich Town	1	2-1	482		S Oldham	Whitehouse 5, Hawkridge 63
Sat Jan 14	A	Gateshead	2	3-1	578	169	S Oldham / M Ryan	Habergham 49, Whitehouse 70, Hawkridge 74
Sat Feb 4	A	Welling United	3	3-1	743		A Quelch	Southwell 8; Ward 49, 51
Sat Feb 25	A	Boreham Wood	4	2-0	901	576	C Hatzidakis	Ward 62, Paine 73 OG
Tue Mar 14	A	York City	SF1	1-2	3,294	1,358	A Backhouse	Angol 14 pen
Sat Mar 18	H	York City	SF2	1-1*	8,409	694	B Toner	Raggett 65

After Extra Time. Lost 2-3 on aggregate.

2016/17 STATISTICS

PLAYER ROLL CALL 2016/17

	TOTAL APPS	GOALS	NATIONAL LEAGUE APPS	GOALS	FA CUP APPS	GOALS	FA TROPHY APPS	GOALS
Paul Farman	58	0	44	0	9	0	5	0
Alex Woodyard	54+3	1	44+1	1	9	0	1+2	0
Sam Habergham	56	4	43	3	9	0	4	1
Matt Rhead	51+5	14	40+3	14	9	0	2+2	0
Luke Waterfall	54+1	7	44	7	9	0	1+1	0
Nathan Arnold	51+3	13	43+2	12	7	1	1+1	0
Sean Raggett	51+1	8	41	5	8	2	2+1	1
Bradley Wood	44+4	2	32+2	2	9	0	3+2	0
Terry Hawkridge	37+9	6	24+8	3	8+1	1	5	2
Alan Power	25+20	4	14+16	2	7+2	2	4+2	0
Jack Muldoon	17+21	3	10+15	3	3+6	0	4	0
Elliott Whitehouse	19+15	6	14+14	4	0	0	5+1	2
Adam Marriott	11+20	4	8+17	4	0+2	0	3+1	0
Harry Anderson	17+13	6	14+12	6	3+1	0	0	0
Theo Robinson	18+4	9	12+2	2	6+1	7	0+1	0
Sean Long	16+4	0	12+2	0	0+2	0	4	0
Lee Beevers	16+1	0	14+1	0	2	0	0	0
Josh Ginnelly	9+8	0	7+6	0	0	0	2+2	0
Billy Knott	10+7	1	8+6	1	0	0	2+1	0
Jamie McCombe	8+7	0	3+4	0	1+3	0	4	0
Lee Angol	13	6	11	5	0	0	2	1
Callum Howe	9+4	0	4+4	0	0	0	5	0
Jonny Margetts	7+4	5	7+3	5	0+1	0	0	0
Macauley Bonne	5+3	1	5+3	1	0	0	0	0
Joe Ward	4+4	3	0+2	0	0+2	0	4	3
Tom Champion	3+2	0	3+2	0	0	0	0	0
Dayle Southwell	3+2	1	2	0	0+1	0	1+1	1
Ross Etheridge	3	0	2	0	0	0	1	0
Riccardo Calder	2	0	1	0	0	0	1	0
Elliot Hodge	0+2	0	0+2	0	0	0	0	0
Alex Simmons	0+2	0	0+2	0	0	0	0	0
Taylor Miles	0+1	0	0+1	0	0	0	0	0

LINCOLN CITY FC

HOME TABLE

	Pld	W	D	L	F	A	GD	Pts
1. LINCOLN CITY	23	17	4	2	48	17	31	55
2. Tranmere	23	16	3	4	43	19	24	51
3. Aldershot Town	23	15	5	3	38	13	25	50
4. Forest Green	23	12	9	2	46	25	21	45
5. Sutton	23	13	6	4	41	25	16	45
6. Dover Athletic	23	13	5	5	48	28	20	44
7. Barrow	23	12	8	3	40	20	20	44
8. Dagenham & R	23	12	5	6	37	28	9	41
9. Gateshead	23	9	9	5	38	23	15	36
10. Bromley	23	11	3	9	33	37	-4	36
11. Wrexham	23	10	5	8	23	24	-1	35
12. Woking	23	9	7	7	32	30	2	34
13. Guiseley	23	9	6	8	32	31	1	33
14. Torquay Utd	23	9	5	9	34	28	6	32
15. Eastleigh	23	8	7	8	28	26	2	31
16. Boreham Wood	23	8	7	8	23	21	2	31
17. Macclesfield	23	9	3	11	30	29	1	30
18. York	23	7	8	8	33	31	2	29
19. Maidstone	23	8	5	10	29	39	-10	29
20. Chester	23	8	3	12	37	35	2	27
21. Solihull Moors	23	8	3	12	35	38	-3	27
22. Southport	23	7	5	11	32	41	-9	26
23. Braintree	23	6	4	13	23	36	-13	22
24. North Ferriby	23	6	2	15	17	40	-23	20

AWAY TABLE

	Pld	W	D	L	F	A	GD	Pts
1. Tranmere	23	13	5	5	36	20	16	44
2. LINCOLN CITY	23	13	5	5	35	23	12	44
3. Dagenham & R	23	14	1	8	42	25	17	43
4. Forest Green	23	13	2	8	42	31	11	41
5. Macclesfield	23	11	5	7	34	28	6	38
6. Dover Athletic	23	11	2	10	37	35	2	35
7. Gateshead	23	10	4	9	34	28	6	34
8. Aldershot Town	23	8	8	7	28	24	4	32
9. Barrow	23	8	7	8	32	33	-1	31
10. Maidstone	23	8	5	10	30	36	-6	29
11. Solihull Moors	23	7	7	9	27	37	-10	28
12. Boreham Wood	23	7	6	10	26	27	-1	27
13. Bromley	23	7	5	11	26	29	-3	26
14. Eastleigh	23	6	8	9	28	37	-9	26
15. Braintree	23	7	5	11	28	40	-12	26
16. Chester	23	6	7	10	26	36	-10	25
17. Wrexham	23	5	8	10	24	37	-13	23
18. Torquay Utd	23	5	6	12	20	33	-13	21
19. York	23	4	9	10	22	39	-17	21
20. Woking	23	5	4	14	34	50	-16	19
21. North Ferriby	23	6	1	16	15	42	-27	19
22. Guiseley	23	4	6	13	18	36	-18	18
23. Sutton	23	2	7	14	20	38	-18	13
24. Southport	23	3	4	16	20	56	-36	13

LINCOLN CITY FOOTBALL CLUB

VANARAMA NATIONAL LEAGUE
CHAMPIONS 2016/17